AWAKEN

TO

YOUR

INHERITANCE

Lynndey Reid

Dedication

This book is dedicated to my husband Chris who has never wavered in his encouragement and support as I share what God has given me. Let's keep going babe!

Endorsements

This exciting new book, Awaken To Your Inheritance, written by Rev. Lynndey Reid, has captured my heart as she has researched, drilled down, and unpacked powerful revelation citing pathways and insights that will change your life and speak to every generation about God's inheritance for you. The treasure of inheritance is both natural and spiritual and this book takes the reader through both the Old and New Testaments, revealing supporting scriptures, while the writer's own personal stories speak to both families and individuals. Lynndey writes about how the discovery of embracing her own inheritance has affected her personal life and family, her ministry, and business. I am convinced, through reading this book, that we all need to take this journey together. It is time to awaken to your inheritance! I recommend that pastors invite Rev. Lynndey Reid to minister in your churches or mission fields in the USA and throughout the world.

Bishop Richard E. Callahan D.Min., D.D.
Founder & President of Proceeding Word Ministries, International and
Maranatha Ministerial Fellowship, International - Orlando, Florida

If you want to know how to step into all that God has for you as His child, this book is for you. You will learn how to gauge what season you are in, how to take down giants, discover your place, your people, and your God given purposes on this earth. Packed full of scripture, revelation, and personal testimony, this book will inspire you to move forward with boldness, stand firm in your identity, and claim your God given inheritance with power and authority. Let Lynndey's heart for God's word awaken you to the promises of God's truth as you courageously possess your promise land!

Tabatha Haines
His Village Church
Culpeper, VA

Awaken To Your Inheritance by Lynndey Reid is a powerful book that will help you on your journey of discovering your God-given inheritance. Did you know that God's inheritance was given to you before you were even born? Did you know you are carriers of His inheritance? Knowing your inheritance will bring clarity and focus to your life.

Once you know your inheritance the spirit of fear will no longer influence your thinking. Follow the blueprint of this book and you will come face to face with your inheritance. If you are lacking purpose in your life, this book is for you, written by a talented author and teacher who brings revelatory knowledge that will awaken your inheritance.

Pastor Brad Keller
Life Coach and Pastor
The Harbor Church
Spicer, MN

Awaken To Your Inheritance will both challenge you and encourage you! Lynndey has succeeded in crafting a book that will make you want to meet the challenges it takes to receive the inheritance that God has for you! Using the Bible and the accounts of some of our heroes in the faith, Lynndey shows how important it is to position ourselves to receive – to take, to "yarash" everything that Jesus died to give us. I also love the way she uses her own life and struggles to make it real. As you read this be open and obedient and see what God does in your life!

Pastor Mike Murray
Catalyst Church on Raceway
Jericho, VT

Let me start by saying I'm all for the ingredients of this book, awakening, inheritance, legacy, freedom, and kingdom. Many times we need to go back in history to understand and grab a hold of our future. Lynndey's passion for this is evident in this book. She desires to see all people understand their identity. Her knowledge of the Bible and its history, bring enlightenment, wisdom, and ultimately awakening. My hope is that this book will cause its readers to have a deeper hunger for all the things God has for them.

Pastor Mark Rampulla
Southview Church
Spring Hill, TN

Table of Contents

How to Use This Book

This book can be used as a personal study, or you can make a small group out of it!

Along with the book, we have ten short video teachings, one to go with each chapter. You can find the videos on our website, www.freeheartscollective.com. Just click the "Videos" button on the upper right hand corner. There you can also view our promo video which you are encouraged to share with others who may also be interested in the study.

Each teaching highlights what is in the chapter and then dives a little deeper into one point. They are meant to complement the chapter, so they won't have the exact information as the chapter, but they are intended to have some overlap.

Thank you for choosing this book. My prayer is that it will be an immense blessing for you!

Lynndey

Other Resources

Please go to our website www.freeheartscollective.com and sign up for our email list to be the first to find out about upcoming events and resources.

Lynndey also co-hosts a podcast called Springs + Roots which you can subscribe to wherever you listen to podcasts.

If you would like to invite Rev. Lynndey to speak at your church or conference, you can contact her via email at freeheartscollective@gmail.com

Introduction

Recently I asked a few friends what comes to your mind when you hear the word inheritance? Here are some of their responses.

> I'm going to get stuff and money
> Receiving a gift that rightfully belongs to me
> Wealth and legacy
> Something passed on from a person who has died

Most people don't think about an inheritance as most people don't expect to receive one. The truth is only a small percentage of people will ever receive any kind of inheritance in this life.

King Hezekiah, was listed as one of the kings that did what was right in the sight of the Lord. Becoming King at twenty five, he immediately went to work turning the nation back towards God. First he tore down the altars of Baal. Then he stood his ground in the face of the King of Assyria when he threatened to destroy Judah. Another time, Hezekiah became so sick he was only inches from dying. Instead of giving up, he cried out to the Lord for mercy. At his petition God granted him fifteen more years of a healthy life.

Soon after God supernaturally spared the nation from their enemies and Hezekiah from death, an envoy of dignitaries came from Babylon to visit the king. News had spread of Israel's wealth and victory over Assyria, the dominant people group of that day. Foolishly King Hezekiah showed the ambassadors ALL of Israel's treasures, holding nothing back, the scripture says. After the visitors left the Lord prompted Isaiah the prophet to question Hezekiah. The king proudly told Isaiah, he showed them everything! God responded through Isaiah saying;

*"Behold the days are coming when all that
is in your house, and what your fathers have
accumulated until this day, shall be carried to
Babylon; nothing shall be left. Says the
LORD. And they shall take away some of your
sons who will descend from you, whom you
will beget, and they shall be eunuchs in the
palace of the King of Babylon.
(2 Kings 20:17-18, NKJV)*

Hezekiah responded;

*"So Hezekiah said to Isaiah," The word of
the LORD which you have spoken is good!"
For he said, "Will there not be peace and truth
at least in my days?" (2 Kings 20:19, NKJV)*

Even though King Hezekiah was a man of great faith, a man
of prayer, a man of obedience, his spiritual eyes weren't open
towards the future. He was unable to see that by showing
Babylon all they had, he was enticing them to come back one
day to plunder Judah. Had Hezekiah seen what Isaiah saw, he
would never have shown the Babylonians the treasures of
Israel!

Notice Isaiah said that Hezekiah showed them *"all that is in
your house, that your fathers have accumulated."* The wealth
Hezekiah so carelessly flaunted was only there because of the
forethought of the previous generations. The wealth he showed
the Babylonians was in fact his inheritance! Sadly, he used the
wealth and prestige his forefathers stored up only for himself,
for his day.

God is not like men; He is not short sighted! God planned
the end from the beginning, not only for all of human history,
but for each one of us. God conceived you in His heart before
you were born. He had a plan for your life which included the

4

greatest gift that He could ever give you, your salvation. At your salvation your body may have looked the same, but the realities of your life changed. You became an eternal being. You came out of the Kingdom of darkness and entered the Kingdom of God. From that moment you became God's child, a member of His royal family, an heir to His Kingdom.

Now you are no longer a slave but God's own child. And since you are his child, God has made you his heir." (Gal. 4:7 NIV)

Having your identity as a child of God anchored in your heart is vitally important for every believer. When I was twenty nine and in desperate need of this revelation myself the Lord helped me settle my identity in Him, once and for all. While in prayer one morning, I saw with my mind's eye a vision of myself. I was a young girl, walking around a fairy tale like Kingdom. I was wearing a pure white dress with intricate designs sown on the edges with gold like thread. As I watched myself in the vision, I noticed other people were staring at me. Their looks weren't mean, is was just as if they each took special notice of me, though I didn't know why. As I was exploring the streets I came to a beautiful royal palace. I stopped to admire a large, wooden, arched door. Without warning the door open to me! There stood Jesus! I was frozen, not knowing what to say or do in His presence. Before I had another thought, He smiled, and waved His hand towards me, inviting me in! In that moment, I knew why people were staring at me. They knew who I was even when I didn't. My dress gave me away! It represented who I am, a daughter of the King.

Before I was born, the Lord chose me. And He wanted me to see myself the way He sees me. I am His child welcomed into His home and He has given me a place in His Kingdom.

5

*Jesus said, "Fear not, little flock; for it is
your Father's good pleasure to give you the
Kingdom." (Luke 12:32, NKJV)*

Just like you and I were in God's heart before we were born,
so was His desire to share His Kingdom with us. Within that
Kingdom is our inheritance! For now our inheritance is
spiritual in nature but in the next age it will come into its
fullness when the spiritual and the natural collide. I can't wait
for that day!

Until then we are carriers and administrators of this great
Kingdom. As such we enjoy measures of the Kingdom realities
here and now. God's love, His forgiveness, His grace, His
empowerment, and His presence are just examples of Kingdom
realities we experience. We live in what some have called, "the
Kingdom tension," the Kingdom is now and its future. It's my
belief that our inheritance is also a Kingdom reality we can
begin to access in this life, and will find its full expression in
the Kingdom age.

*"In Him also we have obtained an
inheritance, being predestined according to
the purpose of Him who works all things to
the counsel of His will"
(Eph. 1:11, NKJV)*

Personally, I've been pursuing this realization of my
inheritance for the last seven years. I've taught on the subject
many times. Every time people are intrigued and want to know
more. After reading this book I believe you will be shocked at
how big the theme of inheritance is in the Bible. I will show you
why I believe that we actually have a part to play in receiving
all that God has set aside for us in the Kingdom, now and in
the future.

Though I hope to show you much, I can't promise to explain
all that your inheritance entails. Even the best of our
understanding is still lacking compared to what will be

revealed at the end of the age. I believe that some portions of our inheritances are the same while others are as unique as each one of us. Since God showed me a glimpse of my inheritance, my whole life has changed! I have more clarity, more focus, and more boldness than ever before. Since pursuing my inheritance I have been set free from a spirit of fear and heard the call of God on my life to teach His word. This revelation of my inheritance in Him has brought me into a whole new place of intimacy with God.

He showed me a type of blueprint that I would like to show to you. It's something that I go back to over and over again, each time I face a new challenge in life. I can't promise that you will experience everything I have if you choose to dive into this subject with me. However, I do know this, your inheritance in His Kingdom is one worth pursuing!

Chapter 1 – Time to Awaken

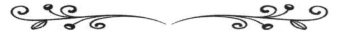

As a child I spent a lot of time with my grandparents. Being one of four children at home, I loved their undivided attention. My grandmother read books to me and would play make-believe with me for hours! "Office," was my favorite thing to play. She always let me be the boss, and she was my assistant, named "Sally Jean." I have many great memories of time spent with my grandparents. One of my favorite things they did was tell me stories about their lives. They were both born before 1920, so their lives sounded more like they took place in a different world than a different generation than mine. I think they considered it part of being a good grandparent to tell me where I came from. Many of their stories still have a special place in my heart today.

My grandfather, Cecil Funkhouser, was born in 1915, his parents were tenant farmers. He was one of eleven children. If you've ever heard the saying, living hand to mouth, that was their life. They ate what they could grow. Their health and livelihood was dependent on the weather. My grandfather didn't reach one hundred pounds until he was fourteen years old. Tenant farming was a hard life to say the least. My grandfather being the oldest boy, dropped out of school in the fourth grade. I guess they needed his two hands, working on the farm, more than having him educated.

One funny story that often came up about my grandfather was his childhood haircuts. The family couldn't afford to go to a barber so instead they would line up all six of the boys in the barn, then one by one, my Great Grandfather would shave their heads with the sheep's shears! Granddaddy, said sometimes it pulled out more than it cut off. Ouch!

My grandparents got married in the middle of the Great Depression. They grew up very poor, similar to their parents before them. They told me, the first few years of their marriage they lived in a chicken coop they converted into a little house. Honestly, I thought they were exaggerating until one day I saw the pictures. They really did live in a chicken coop! They just did what they needed to do to survive.

Like many in his generation, my Grandfather was drafted into World War II. His first assignment was to drive one of the generals to and from various places. On numerous occasions, the general's jeep broke down en route. As it turned out, my grandfather had a knack for working on car engines. He was always able to figure out the problem and get the jeep running again. After fixing the general's jeep several times, the general put my grandfather in charge of the entire motor pool.

In 1946, my grandfather made it home safe from the war. With his newly found interest in auto-mechanics he eventually landed a job at a local garage. Within a few years my grandparents saved enough money to purchase a piece of property in order to build their first home. Only they didn't just build a house, they also built an auto mechanic shop, right next to it. They called it, Funkhouser's Garage. With my grandmother, doing the books, and my grandfather repairing cars, their business was successful for thirty years.

Growing up in that same town, even though it is unusual, everyone knew my last name because of my grandparents' garage. They had a reputation for being honest and fair. I was told there were a few times they forgave the debts of customers who were unable to pay due to difficult circumstances. My grandparents were very special people. They both had extremely humble beginnings but because of their hard work, foresight, and love for their family, when they died they left an inheritance for their children.

It was while writing this book, I witnessed my dad receive his portion of the inheritance. It was exactly what my grandparents wanted it to be, a huge blessing. The blessing of the inheritance didn't just stop with my dad. My parents decided to share the gift. Upon receipt they gave a portion of my grandparent's inheritance to each one of their children and grandchildren. They shared it with nineteen people in all. The inheritance my grandparents worked hard for became a blessing to three generations after them.

> *"A good man leaves an inheritance to his children's children..." (Prov. 13:22, NKJV)*

Now, I must ask you, if a good man leaves an inheritance for his children, how much more of an inheritance do you think your Heavenly Father has for you?

IT'S TIME TO AWAKEN TO YOUR INHERITANCE!

After Jesus' ascension and the day of Pentecost, at which three thousand men and women came to believe that Jesus was Israel's Messiah, the newborn church began to explode. The first chapters of the book of Acts contain awesome phrases every believer would love to hear were happening in their community, like; "then the number of disciples was multiplying," and there were "great signs and wonders among the people," and " believers were increasingly added to the Lord, multitudes both men and women." What an awesome time to have lived in Jerusalem. But with the spreading of the knowledge of Jesus as Messiah among the people, so came with it, persecution.

> *At that time a great persecution arose against the church which was at Jerusalem; and they were all scattered throughout the*

regions of Judea and Samaria...
(Acts 8:1 NKJV)

One certain, young zealous Pharisee named Saul, made it his personal mission to join the persecution and rid the nation of any remembrance of the imposter named Jesus. As Saul was "breathing threats and murder against the disciples of the Lord," He gained written permission to travel to Damascus with the intent of dragging any believers in Jesus he found back to Jerusalem to stand trial and possible execution.

As Saul's caravan traveled the main road from Jerusalem to Damascus, a brilliant light suddenly shone down on them like a spotlight in the desert sky. At the light, Saul fell to his knees, while those with him ran away in fear. A thunderous voice spoke from the light saying, "Saul, Saul, why are you persecuting Me?" Saul, responded, "Who are You, Lord?" That night, the resurrected Messiah made Himself known to Saul, saying " I am Jesus, whom you are persecuting...." During that life altering encounter Jesus gave Saul his life mission, of which the effects are still being felt in the church today. Jesus said;

> *"I will deliver you from the Jewish people,*
> *as well as from the Gentiles, to whom I now*
> *send you, 'to open their eyes, in order to turn*
> *them from darkness to light, and from the*
> *power of Satan to God, that they may receive*
> *forgiveness of sins and an inheritance among*
> *those who are sanctified by faith in Me."*
> *(Acts 26 :17-18, NKJV)*

This night marked the beginning of Saul turning all that rage against Jesus and His church, to a passionate lifelong pursuit of seeking to know Him. Saul later became known as the Apostle Paul. He became one of the most influential believers of all times. His life and instructions to believers through the epistles of the New Testament have become a treasure of wisdom and knowledge for the church then and now. Paul spent the remainder of his life going around the known world sharing the good news Jesus told him to. Paul founded many of the churches mentioned in the New Testament, and ultimately gave his life for the sake of the gospel.

Did you notice, Jesus' mission for this significant man? He said, tell them about the forgiveness of sins, and that they have an inheritance. I have often wondered why Jesus would call a Pharisee, a man who practically had the Old Testament memorized, to the mission of sharing about the New Covenant. But God always knows what He is doing. When Jesus told Saul, tell them about the forgiveness of sins and an inheritance, Saul knew exactly what Jesus was talking about. As a Hebrew man there were two things he understood. First, he needed to have his sins forgiven. Second, he wanted to take his rightful place in the land of his inheritance.

As the church we have long understood the foreshadowing of the Old Testament sacrifices pointing us towards the ultimate sacrifice Jesus made on the cross. Yet I would like to propose to you, there is yet another major theme the Old Testament foreshadows. It's our inheritance! I'm sure you have heard about the forgiveness of sins, but what have you heard about your inheritance?

Even though the subject of our inheritance hasn't held the main stage in church teachings, I believe this is the season that the Lord will begin revealing the importance of learning about our inheritance more and more. Salvation is only the beginning, the first step of our journey. Pursuing our inheritance is the second, it's the reason we continue living this life on earth after our salvation. My desire is that this book will act as a foundation upon which you will search God out further to know what your inheritance holds.

SUNDAY SCHOOL CORRECTIONS

If you grew up in Sunday School like me you probably learned a lot of catchy little songs that were a lot of fun to sing. As a kid, we sang songs about the walls of Jericho falling down, of Father Abraham who had many sons, and crossing the Jordan to get to the Promised Land. These fun songs were meant to teach children the stories of the Bible.

In a couple of the old songs crossing the Jordan was meant to symbolize death, and the Promised Land heaven. Eventually somebody pointed out that comparing crossing the Jordan to death was incorrect, and that the Promised Land couldn't represent heaven because in heaven we won't have any giants to face or battles to fight.

If we take our Sunday School corrections one step further, they will open up another paradigm when it comes to the land of Israel. Did you know the title "The Promised Land" never actually occurs in the Hebrew text? It is called the land of promise many, many times, which is why the phrase The Promised Land was probably adopted. There is certainly nothing wrong with calling it The Promised Land, however in doing so we have come to think of it by the title, instead of what it is actually called in scripture, over and over again and that is, their inheritance!

The land of Israel is referred to as the Hebrew's inheritance, or a land they are to inherit well over two hundred times! The land is more than a piece of property, to the Hebrew people, it's their God given inheritance. Their inheritance is a holy place, set apart just for them to live in, for the purpose of fulfilling God's will in their lives. Look at these passages and notice how God, Abraham, Moses, David, and Solomon referred to the land of Israel.

God spoke these words to Abraham the night He made a covenant with him:

> *Then He said to him, "I am the LORD, who*
> *brought you out of Ur of the Chaldeans, to*
> *give you this land **to inherit it.**"*
> *(Gen. 15:7, NKJV)*

Moses said this to God as He was interceding for the children of Israel after they sinned by worshipping the golden calf:

> *"Remember Abraham, Isaac, and Israel,*
> *Your servants, to whom You swore by Your*
> *own self, and said to them, 'I will multiply*
> *your descendants as the stars of heaven; and*
> *all this land that I have spoken of **I give to***
> ***your descendants, and they shall inherit it***
> ***forever.**' (Ex. 32:13, NKJV)*

David, questioned King Saul's motive for chasing him:

> *Now let my lord the king listen to his*
> *servant's words. If the LORD has incited you*
> *against me, then may he accept an offering. If,*
> *however, people have done it, may they be*
> *cursed before the LORD! **They have driven me***
> ***today from my share in the LORD's***
> ***inheritance** and have said, 'Go, serve other*
> *gods.' (1 Sam. 26:19, NIV)*

King Solomon stood before the altar and dedicated the temple and said :

> *"When the heavens are shut and there is*
> *no rain because they have sinned against You,*
> *when they pray toward this place and confess*
> *Your name, and turn from their sin because*
> *You afflict them, then hear in heaven and*
> *forgive the sin of Your servants, Your people*

Israel, that You may teach them the good way
in which they should walk; and send rain on
*Your land **which You have given to Your***
people as an inheritance."
(1 Kings 8:35-36, NKJV)

THE LAND OF ISRAEL

The reason I have come to the conclusion that our inheritance is such a huge deal to God, is because of how much of the storyline of the thirty-nine books of the Old Testament revolve around the land of Israel. Think about it, whether or not the children of Israel will possess their inheritance dominates the Old Testament narrative.

Genesis holds the promise of inheritance

God called Abraham out of Ur to the land of Canaan. Once there God promised the land as an inheritance to Abraham's future descendants, not once, not twice, but five times! After Abraham's death God renewed the promise of the inheritance to Abraham's son, Isaac, and again with his grandson, Jacob.

Exodus, Leviticus, Numbers, Deuteronomy & Joshua

These five books tell the supernatural story of the children of Israel's journey to claim their promised inheritance. And God's instructions on how to live in a way that they could maintain the land, once they possessed it.

Judges

Tells the story of the first several hundred years of Abraham's family in the land of their inheritance. It shows their struggle to keep it and rule over it under the system of judges and priests.

1 & 2nd Samuel, 1 & 2nd Kings, 1 & 2nd Chronicles

These six books contain the stories of the establishment of a kingly dynasty in Israel, their successes and failures. The people were in a constant battle with the surrounding people groups to maintain their inheritance. Just like God promised them before they entered the land, their right to possess their inheritance was based on whether or not they were following Him.

The Major and Minor Prophets

The prophetic books carry messages of warning to Israel, if they would not remain faithful to God, they would no longer have the right to live in the land of their inheritance. They also hold the promise of the Messiah, the New Covenant, and the future blessings God would bestow on His people based on His faithfulness, not on theirs.

Ezra & Nehemiah

God orchestrates it so that a remnant of Jews were released from captivity to once again live in the land of their inheritance. Under the leadership of Ezra, Nehemiah and Zerubbabel, God instructed them to rebuild the walls of Jerusalem and the temple. Though they took up residence in the land of their inheritance, at this time, the Jews were not allowed to govern the land. Them living in the land and the rebuilding of the temple and the walls were a down payment and a foreshadowing of the future promise of the full redemption of the inheritance that will be seen at the end of the age.

BRINGING IT ALL TOGETHER

The writer of Hebrews calls the law of sacrifices in the Old Testament a shadow of what the New Covenant would hold, the forgiveness of sins. Likewise, I believe the children of Israel's inheritance in the land of Israel foreshadows the spiritual inheritance God's children can enjoy in His Kingdom. The forgiveness of sins and inheritance go together.

It was with intentionality that God filled up the Old Testament with this idea that His people should live in the land of their inheritance. Their journey to possess it parallels our journey to possess the inheritance God has for us in this life which will come into its fullness in the next. Just like their walk with God towards their inheritance was one worth taking, so is ours!

CHAPTER 1 — QUESTIONS

1. In what ways does thinking about the Promised Land as symbolic of your spiritual inheritance open up a new paradigm for you?

2. Why do you think so much of the Old Testament scriptures center around the children of Israel's promised inheritance and whether they would live in it or not?

3. What have you heard about your spiritual inheritance?

4. What specifically about your inheritance are you hoping to learn from this book?

1. If you received a phone call like Lynndey described, saying you were receiving an enormous natural inheritance, how would it change your everyday outlook?

2. In what ways do you think understanding the fullness of your spiritual inheritance could change your outlook in a similar way?

3. Why do you think Jesus paired redemption and inheritance when He commissioned Paul that night on the road to Damascus?

Chapter 2 – The Journey of A Lifetime

When my two youngest boys were in third and fourth grade, I homeschooled them. Every day during physical science class I couldn't help but stop mid-lesson to express my awe at how perfectly God created nature in order to reflect the spiritual truths of His Kingdom. After a while, it was a running joke between the boys as to how long each day my detour would take!

At that time, I didn't understand why the boys didn't join with me in my wonder. Why couldn't they see what I saw? I came to realize that as ten and eleven-year-old boys they needed to learn the natural things of this world first before they could understand the spiritual truths creation reflects. Like the scripture says, first the natural, and then the spiritual.

FIRST THE NATURAL AND THEN THE SPIRITUAL

> *However, the spiritual is not first but the natural, and afterward the spiritual.*
> *(1 Cor. 15:46, NKJV)*

During His earthly ministry, this is the way Jesus taught as well. He used the natural world to explain the spiritual truths, we call them parables. For most of the parables, Jesus, left it up to the hearers as to whether they would press into the deeper spiritual meaning the natural stories held. This way of teaching spiritual truths through natural things did not begin with Jesus' ministry, it began in the Old Testament. The entirety of the Old Testament's natural accounts were written

20

for the church to learn spiritual truths from. While writing to the Corinthian church, Paul highlight's the children of Israel's journey from Egypt to their inheritance as an account that we need to take special notice of.

> *I don't want you to forget, dear brothers and sisters, about our ancestors in the wilderness long ago. All of them were guided by a cloud that moved ahead of them, and all of them walked through the sea on dry ground. In the cloud and in the sea, all of them were baptized as followers of Moses. All of them ate the same spiritual food, and all of them drank the same spiritual water. For they drank from the spiritual rock that traveled with them, and that rock was Christ. Yet God was not pleased with most of them, and their bodies were scattered in the wilderness. These things happened as a warning to us, so that we would not crave evil things as they did.......... These things happened to them as examples for us. They were written down to warn us who live at the end of the age.*
> *(1 Cor. 10:1-11, NLT)*

Just as Jesus left it up to the hearers of His parables to go beyond the natural and look for the spiritual meaning behind the stories, I believe it is the same for the children of Israel's story. That is what this book is all about, learning from this dramatic account of the children of Israel's trek from Egypt to their inheritance. Like Paul, said, it was written for us!

Even though you and I may not see ourselves as walking through a wilderness or crossing a sea, we still face the same types of temptations the children of Israel did. The path they took from Egypt to their inheritance contains a road map for us today if we are willing to follow it. Each physical place they traveled represents a significant spiritual place for us on our journey towards our inheritance that begins at salvation.

THE JOURNEY OF ALL TIMES

More than any other, the generation freed from Egypt must own the bragging rights for seeing the most supernatural events of all time! They witnessed God rain down ten nation shattering plagues on Egypt, which ended with the death of every first-born child and animal. They stood before the Red Sea as it divided so they could cross over on dry ground. In the wilderness, God gave them water from a rock to drink, and when they were hungry, he sent manna and quail to eat. As if that wasn't enough, God Himself descended on Mt. Sinai as they camped at its base! No other people group has ever lived through such supernatural events as the generation set free from Egypt.

Their journey began when they were freed from their slavery in *Egypt*. After which, God led them through a season I'm calling *the wilderness crossing* that included camping at the foot of Mt. Sinai for around a year. The next stop, the edge of their *inheritance*! At the report of giants in the land, the people were unwilling to go any further. At their refusal, God turned them back around into *the wilderness of wandering,* where they went in circles for about forty years.

After all the first generation died natural deaths in the wilderness, the Lord brought the next generation once again back to the borders of their inheritance. Under the leadership of Joshua, the second generation did what their parents would not and fought giants in order to possess their promised inheritance.

This is the roadmap the Apostle Paul highlighted for our learning: *Egypt > Wilderness Crossing > Inheritance > Wilderness Wandering*

EGYPT = BONDAGE

As we jump into the Hebrews' story in the book of Exodus, we find the young nation in a place where Abraham would never have wanted them to be, in bondage. With God's permission around four hundred years before the book of Exodus opens, Abraham's grandson, Jacob, led his family to Egypt. They went there to reconnect with his eleventh son Joseph, and to escape a famine in the land of Canaan. At that time, the Hebrew family was seventy people in all. The small family quickly grew into the multitude of people God promised Abraham they would be.

But the Israelites were exceedingly fruitful;
they multiplied greatly, increased in numbers
and became so numerous that the land was
filled with them. (Ex.1:7, NIV)

As the number of Hebrews continued to rapidly increase, the Egyptians became afraid of them, thinking if a war came, they would fight against them. Driven by their fear, they enslaved the Hebrew people. The scripture describes their slavery as crushing, cruel, and brutal. But to the Egyptians disgust, the more they afflicted the Hebrews the more they grew in number!

So they put slave masters over them to
oppress them with forced labor..... But the
more they were oppressed, the more they
multiplied and spread; so, the Egyptians came
to dread the Israelites and worked them
ruthlessly. They made their lives bitter with
harsh labor in brick and mortar and with all
kinds of work in the fields; in all their harsh
labor the Egyptians worked them ruthlessly.
(Ex. 1:7-14, NIV)

Though, Abraham, would have never wanted his family to be slaves, God, foretold him they would be. On the night God made a covenant with Abraham, God said *"Know certainly that*

23

your descendants will be strangers in a land that is not theirs, and will serve them and they will afflict them for four hundred years." (Gen. 15:13-14) God not only foreknew it, He was the One who planned it, telling Abraham's grandson Jacob, to go down into Egypt.

You may wonder why would God put His covenant family in this situation? The answer is revealed once you take a step back and look at the scene God was setting. God sent His people to Egypt, knowing they would become slaves, because God is a masterful playwright. Through His covenant people's slavery, He was setting the stage for their dramatic exodus from Egypt. Their exodus was filled with so much awe, that it became famous throughout the ancient world. It was so awesome the account is still widely known today. Even unbelievers worldwide know about the ten plagues brought down on Egypt thousands of years ago. God's display of love and power made all the world see that Yahweh, the God of the Hebrews is the only One who can save!

God wanted us to see their story, because their story is the same story lived out by the whole human race. The Hebrew family didn't start out in slavery. Their father Abraham was not only free but also very rich. *"Abraham was very rich in livestock, in silver, and in gold' (Gen. 13:2).* The Hebrews' family began the same way all humanity began. Just like Abraham, Adam and Eve were also wealthy and free. They were so free they walked around naked, and so rich they were given the world to have dominion over. Yet, because of their choice to disobey God, sin entered the world.

Sin and death robbed Adam and Eve of their wealth and freedom like the slavery of Egypt robbed Abraham's family of their wealth and freedom. Adam and Eve's story runs parallel to the story of the Hebrew nation. They began in freedom and riches through their father Abraham but ended up as slaves in Egypt in need of salvation. In God's mercy, He orchestrated for His covenant nation to become the slaves of Egypt, to show you

24

and I the true spiritual state of mankind. Though God meant us to be free and rich at our creation, humanity is plagued with the curse of sin and death. Man's sinful nature is so powerful, we are forced to obey its desires, just like the Hebrews were forced to obey their Egyptian taskmasters.

> *Wherefore, as by one man sin entered into the world, and death by sin; and so death passed upon all men, for that all have sinned:*
> *(Rom. 5:12, NKJV)*

> *For the wages of sin is death...*
> *(Rom. 6:23, NKJV)*

IT ALL STARTS WITH A CRY

At the height of the Hebrews slavery, they began to cry out, to the God of their father Abraham for salvation.

> *....Then the children of Israel groaned because of the bondage, and they cried out; and their cry came up to God because of the bondage*
> *(Ex. 2:23, NKJV)*

Salvation for each one of us began the same way it did for the Hebrews. Our eyes were open to the mastery that sin had over our lives, and we longed to be free. Just like God already had a plan in motion to send Moses, God already had a plan in motion to send His Son into the world to save whoever would come to Him. *Jesus, is the Lamb slain from the foundation of the world (Rev. 13:8, NKJV).*

Under Moses' leadership, the Hebrews exodus from Egypt under the blood of the Passover Lamb is a beautiful symbolic picture of our salvation. Just like God rescued the children of Israel from the slavery of Egypt, He will rescue all who choose

25

to come under the redeeming blood of His Son, Jesus. God delivered His chosen people from the occultic polytheistic worship of the Egyptian gods so they could freely worship Him, the One True God. He brought them out of a land of darkness to live in a new Kingdom with Him as their light. Their exodus is a natural picture of a spiritual reality that happens to us at salvation. At salvation, we literally come out of the bondage of sin and death and enter the Kingdom of God.

For he has rescued us from the Kingdom of darkness and transferred us into the Kingdom of his dear Son (Col. 1:13, NLT)

Leaving the bonds of Egypt was just the beginning for the Hebrew nation. God had a journey ahead for His people with a final destination in mind. He brought them out of Egypt for the same reason He brought you and I out from under the slavery of sin, because He has something good for you! God has a place for you to live in His peace, and a place where you can expand His Kingdom in this life. It's called your inheritance!

Your inheritance includes a place of maintained freedom, a place for you to exercise your God given authority in the earth, it's a place of fruitful multiplication! Your inheritance includes all of the things, the land of Israel included for the children of Israel. The only thing is, just like for the children of Israel, there is something to cross over to get there.

THE WILDERNESS & MT. SINAI

As they left behind the slavery of Egypt to go to their own land it must have felt like a dream. I can only imagine the excitement they felt, to be finally be free. With all the excitement, I wonder how long it took them before they realized, they didn't know where they were going! Just like their father Abraham, theirs would be a journey of faith to get to the land of their inheritance.

26

The scripture says the children of Israel left Egypt with boldness. It wasn't long before that boldness would be tested. Within three days, Pharaoh regretted his decision to let them go, so he led his army along with six hundred chariots out with the intention of dragging the Hebrews back into their bondage. Ever notice how those things that have held us in bondage always want to drag us back under their mastery, even after a mighty defeat?

> When the king of Egypt was told that the people had fled, Pharaoh and his officials changed their minds about them and said, "What have we done? We have let the Israelites go and have lost their services!" So he had his chariot made ready and took his army with him. He took six hundred of the best chariots, along with all the other chariots of Egypt, with officers over all of them. **The Lord hardened the heart of Pharaoh king of Egypt, so that he pursued the Israelites,** who were marching out boldly. (Ex. 14:5-8, NIV)

Did you see that? It was God who hardened Pharaoh's heart so that he would try to reclaim the Hebrews as his slaves. It was God that took the children of Israel by the way of the wilderness, putting them in a vulnerable position. And it was God who put their backs up to the Red Sea, essentially making them Egyptian bait!

Why would God allow His people to be in this terrible situation, ON PURPOSE? The answer to that question is, He was testing them. Held in between their new found freedom and their precious inheritance were the trials and tests of the wilderness crossing. This is what the wilderness crossing symbolizes the trials and tests we go through in life.

Having their backs up against the Red Sea and Pharaoh at their door was just the first of many bad situations the children of Israel found themselves in during the wilderness crossing. Three days after they left Egypt, they had no water to drink. About six weeks after they left Egypt, they started running out of food. As if all that wasn't enough, the Amalekites attacked them. If I were them, I would have started asking the question, "Am I following God or the Devil?"

Here is what we need to come to terms with as believers, just because we are following God doesn't mean things will always be easy. In fact, when we are following God, we will go through seasons of trials and testings.

Let me ask you, are you praying for more of the Lord in your life? Are you asking Him for open doors to minister? Are you looking for more Kingdom opportunities? I bet you are, you've probably even prayed a prayer similar to this, "Lord, show me the path you have for my life." The truth is God wants to lead you on that path and give you a greater measure of things in His Kingdom, here and now. But because He is a wise and good father, He needs to know we are ready to handle greater responsibility and greater challenges.

Like the tests you took in school, any test God allows to come your way is to see what you know, to see what you believe. Tests are meant to reveal specifically what you believe about God and yourself. The Lord said to the children of Israel:

> *"And you shall remember that the LORD*
> *your God led you all the way these forty years*
> *in the wilderness, to humble you and test you,*
> *to know what was in your heart...*
> *(Deut. 8:2, NKJV)*

The purpose of things within our hearts coming to light is not for God's knowledge, *"For He knows the secrets of the heart"* (Psalm 44:21), it's for ours. As the creator of the human heart, God knows we won't live beyond what is hidden in our hearts. If we don't believe God in a certain area of our lives it will limit us in ways He never intended, remember complete and total freedom is our original design.

At times we all struggle with wrong beliefs about God. The good news is, He isn't offended, He just wants to use seasons of wilderness crossings to get those wrong beliefs out of our hearts and the truth in! It's up to us whether we will let the testing do its work. I could take you to certain years of my life, where God was correcting wrong beliefs I had that I didn't even know were there until through a trial, He revealed them to me. I used to believe that He didn't really have good things for me, that He was always disappointed in me, and that I had to earn His love through performance. None of those things are true about God, but I unknowingly believed them all, until a time of testing came, and my true feelings were revealed. As I confessed the wrong beliefs revealed through those seasons, the Holy Spirit helped me come into agreement with the truth of who God really is. Confession is like a stake you put in the ground and hold onto as you turn yourself back toward the truth.

Even though the children of Israel were free from Egypt, they carried with them limiting beliefs about God. It can be the same for us after salvation. Though God has saved us we still need many "change of minds" to live the life He's called us to. It's here in the wilderness crossing of Sinai that God met them, with trials and testing designed to help them reform their thoughts about themselves and God. The trials and tests we face in life are meant for the same purpose, to change us from the inside out.

My brethren, count it all joy when you fall into various trials, knowing that the testing of your faith produces patience. But let patience have its perfect work, that you may be perfect and complete, lacking nothing.
(Jas. 1:2-4, NKJV)

In all this you greatly rejoice, though now
for a little while you may have had to suffer
grief in all kinds of trials. These have come so
that the proven genuineness of your faith—of
greater worth than gold, which perishes even
though refined by fire—may result in praise,
glory and honor when Jesus Christ is
revealed. (1 Pet.1:6-7, NIV)

God sees farther ahead in the journey than we do. He knows what it's going to take to enter into our inheritance. Trials aren't meant to take us out, they are meant to make us stronger! Next time you are in a trial, just stop and ask God, "What wrong beliefs have I come into agreement with about You or myself?" Listen for His voice, He will gently tell you any areas you are believing that are false about Him or you. Confess the wrong beliefs, and then begin to declare the truth of who God has said He is, and who He says you are.

ON TO SINAI

Eleven days after they left Egypt, God brought the children of Israel to camp at the foot of Mt. Sinai. God descended on the mountain, and Moses went up. From the mountain top God began to give the people their new identity. *God said: "And ye shall be unto me a Kingdom of priests, and a holy nation." (Ex. 19:6, NKJV)*

The nation of Israel was to be a people set apart for God's purposes in the earth. As His kings they were to be God's royal ambassadors making His will known in the earth through His word. As His priests they were to have one hand extended toward heaven and the other reaching out to mankind. As a light to the world, they were to be a representation of God and His Kingdom. This is the second purpose of the wilderness crossing, to know our identity.

Their exodus from Egypt physically freed them from slavery, but their pass-through Sinai was meant to free their minds from slavery. Our identities are hugely impacted by the words spoken over our lives. Though this generation had been brought up to hear they were only good for overworking, abusing and cruelty, God wanted to impart to them their real identity based on what He said about them.

Sadly, we often find like the children of Israel that the words spoken over us from our parents, siblings and peers leave us with an identity much lower than the one God has for us. When we get saved, or leave Egypt, God wants to impart our true identity to us as His children. It's in the secluded places of the wilderness crossing that we can listen to God's words over our lives, and begin to find our true identities in Him.

> *"For you died, and your life is now hidden*
> *with Christ in God." (Col. 3:3, NIV)*

It's in the wilderness crossing seasons that we have the opportunity to grow the most! The wilderness crossing is a time to let God make the crooked places straight, to satisfy us with spiritual food and water that will change us from the inside out. It's the place where God helps us increase our faith in who He is, and impart to us our identity in Him. The point of any wilderness crossing we go through in life, is for the same purpose God had for the children of Israel. He was preparing them to enter their inheritance! I know most Christians panic when they hear the word wilderness. But believe it or not, the wilderness crossing is a good place to be.

THE LAND OF CANAAN, THEIR INHERITANCE

After leaving Egypt, and crossing the wilderness comes inheritance. From the time they left Egypt until they got to the edge of their inheritance was a little under two years. Unfortunately, the generation of adults who left Egypt did not enter into their promised inheritance. At the report of giants in the land, they refused to move forward. However, that was not God's will for them, His will was for them to begin to enjoy what He had set apart for them. We must never forget that though God is sovereign over the world, He has given man the gift of free choice.

God will not make us do anything. He has promised to lead us and to guide us, to be with us, but He never promised to force us to do something we are unwilling to! Though this generation did not enter their inheritance, God never left them. His presence was still there seen in the cloud and the fire. His provision didn't stop either. He provided manna for them all forty years they wandered. What did happen is something that happens too many times for believers, they only got a glimpse of their promised inheritance. They never got to experience the goodness of it.

Awakening to your inheritance, is about seeing the promises of God for your life and walking in them. The children of Israel were meant to live in their inheritance and so are you and I. This book is an effort to help you see your inheritance, move toward it and possess it in this life.

By walking in your inheritance, you will be doing the same things the children of Israel were supposed to do in their inheritance. Not only will you be establishing the Kingdom of God in your sphere of influence, but you will also be dispossessing the enemy from positions that he has long held. Heaven will invade earth through you as you take the place and portion God has reserved for you in this life. I've reserved an entire chapter to talk about the land of Israel and how it symbolizes our inheritance. But for now, I want to focus your attention on seeing the path God intended for them.

EGYPT > WILDERNESS CROSSING > INHERITANCE

Egypt, the wilderness crossing, and possessing your inheritance are more than just a one-time journey. I believe they should be seen as part of a healthy cycle believers will go through many times in life, while pursuing God's promises for our lives. Let me explain.

Though their deliverance from Egypt represents our eternal salvation, it also represents all the areas in our lives after salvation God wants to deliver us from. The Greek word for salvation, sotiría, conveys a continuing salvation. It doesn't mean that we are continually being saved into God's family, but that we are continually being saved, healed, and delivered from sin's stronghold's or types of "Egypt's" in our lives. There will be seasons in life, that we come out of types of "Egypt."

When I say there are times in our lives that we are delivered out of types of "Egypt's", I must reaffirm that when Jesus died, rose, and ascended He won a complete victory. Us coming out of any other types of "Egypt" are **NEVER** about Jesus needing to defeat sin, death, and the grave again. Coming out of a type of "Egypt" is about us, coming into agreement with the victory He has already won on our behalf. It's when we are awakened to areas of bondage, that we can confess and repent by applying

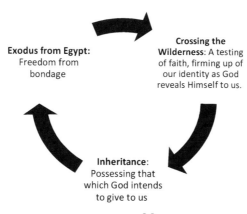

Exodus from Egypt:
Freedom from bondage

Crossing the Wilderness: A testing of faith, firming up of our identity as God reveals Himself to us.

Inheritance: Possessing that which God intends to give to us the blood of the Lamb to the sin, then we will exit every "Egypt" and walk in the freedom He has already secured for us.

Just like leaving Egypt is part of a cycle so are seasons of wilderness crossings. These are the seasons you feel like your back is against the sea and your enemy is closing in. It's in those times you know you're following God, but you just don't know where you're going. These are the harder times of life, but if we lean into them, we can learn a greater dependency of God, and experience a deeper intimacy with Him, that will strengthen our faith like at no other time. The more mature we become the easier it is to navigate these seasons and teach others how to do the same.

> *Brethren, do not be children in*
> *understanding; however, in malice be babes,*
> *but in understanding be mature.*
> *(1Cor. 14:20, NKJV)*

I have gone through this cycle of exiting Egypt, crossing a wilderness and on to inheritance many times. A few years ago, the ministry that God had birthed through me was going great, I was walking in portions of an inheritance God had for me. What I didn't know was that hidden deep inside my heart were some areas of pride. Pride is a type of Egypt because it binds you up and prevents you from experiencing the freedom that humility offers. I wasn't in any overt sin, quite the contrary, I was following God's leadership in my life. Nevertheless, I was having some really hard times in some very important relationships in my life. It was time to cycle through the seasons again.

For a while God took me out from a season of experiencing the goodness of inheritance, because He wanted me to walk out of the "Egypt" of pride. I remember talking to the Lord about the troubles I was having one morning. I said to Him over and over again. "How can they treat me this way?" "I don't deserve this!" The Holy Spirit gently replayed my words, to me and I could see the emphasis my complaints had on I and me. I felt the Lord, say to me, "Lynndey, look at how I was treated. Are you better than Me?" Jesus said no disciple is above their teacher, if they treated Him a certain way, people would treat us that way too. I was awaken to the "Egypt" of pride in my life and began to ask God to forgive me and make me more like Him.

Pride says I need people to think of me and value me a certain way. Humility says I know what God thinks about me, and from that place I can freely love others without regard to how they treat me. God wanted me to learn that my value is not based on what other people think about me, but in who He calls me daughter. God was calling me higher by asking me to go lower, where only He could see. God wanted to set me free from pride, or at least the degree that He was showing me at that time. After leaving that "Egypt" I went through a wilderness crossing, where I was tested many times, to see if I would continue to walk in the humility Jesus was calling me to.

When I've experienced seasons of inheritance, it's usually a culmination of seasons, where I am walking out everything I've learned from the last two seasons of Egypt and the wilderness crossing. Every season that I've walked in more of my inheritance, is defined by sustained growth or a new normal in God. I see these three places of our journey as a longer description of the glory to glory cycle. Even though you may not think about Egypt and the wilderness crossing as glorious they are! Every time we leave a prison door that has been opened by Jesus final work on the cross, God gets the glory. Every time we walk through a wilderness crossing and come out strengthen with power and might in our inner man, God gets the glory. Every time we walk in new places of maintaining those freedoms, and expanding the authority and dominion God has given us, you guessed it, GOD GETS THE GLORY!

JESUS WENT THROUGH THE SAME CYCLE

One of the things I love about walking with Jesus is that whenever life presents me with a challenge, I know that all I need to do is look to Him. I know that somewhere, somehow Jesus went through what I'm going through, and that gives me hope. During His earthly life Jesus went through this same cycle of a type of Egypt, a wilderness crossing and then onto to claiming His inheritance.

Though Jesus **NEVER** sinned He did in one way experience a type of Egypt.

> *But made himself of no reputation, and*
> *took upon him the form of a servant, and was*
> *made in the likeness of men*
> *(Phil. 2:7, NKJV)*

Jesus, the great I Am, gave up His heavenly state so that He could come to earth and live as a man. Becoming a human and living on the earth was a type of Egypt for Jesus. He lived among us and though He never sinned he was fully immersed in this world. So often we see Jesus groaning within Himself at people's pain, suffering, and even death, three things God did not create. Not only did God limit Himself in a human form, He also put Himself through the cycles of humanity coming as a child and subjecting Himself to his parents will.

> *Then He went down with them and came to*
> *Nazareth, and was subject to them...*
> *(Luke 2:51, NKJV)*

Jesus limiting Himself to humanity, it's natural cycles, and subjecting Himself to the will of His parents was a type of Egypt. He left the Egypt of being under His parents when He began His ministry, which scholars believe was around the age of thirty. He began his ministry by being baptized by His cousin John.

Then Jesus came from Galilee to John at
the Jordan to be baptized by him.
(Matt. 3:13, NKJV)

As He came out of the water, the Holy Spirit filled Him. Immediately, He was led by the Spirit into the wilderness. It's the same pattern as the children of Israel. First they left Egypt, then they were baptized through the Red Sea, then into the wilderness where they would be tested.

Then Jesus was led by the Spirit into the
wilderness to be tempted by the Devil. After
fasting forty days and forty nights, he was
hungry. (Matt. 4:1-2, NIV)

In the wilderness, Jesus was tested just like His forefathers. He allowed Himself to be hungry and thirsty just like them. Though the enemy pressed Jesus on every side He passed every test. Even when He was alone and hungry, surrounded by enemies, He never wavered in His confidence in God's provision and protection. Though the enemy pounded on His identity, and continually questioned Him, *"If you really are the Son of God....."* Jesus knew who He was and didn't need to prove it to the Devil or anyone else! The question Jesus faced in the wilderness was the same for the Israelites, and for you and I. When times get tough, will we still believe God is God?

Jesus came out of the wilderness the same way God wants every one of us to come out of wilderness crossings, STRONGER IN THE SPIRIT!

When the Devil had finished all this
tempting, he left him until an opportune time.
Jesus returned to Galilee in the power of the
Spirit, and news about him spread throughout
the whole countryside.
(Luke 4:13-15, NIV)

Immediately after coming out of the wilderness, He began to claim part of His inheritance! Our freedom!

> *He went to Nazareth, where he had been*
> *brought up, and on the Sabbath day he went*
> *into the synagogue, as was his custom. He*
> *stood up to read, and the scroll of the prophet*
> *Isaiah was handed to him. Unrolling it, he*
> *found the place where it is written: "The Spirit*
> *of the Lord is on me, because he has anointed*
> *me to proclaim good news to the poor. He has*
> *sent me to proclaim freedom for the prisoners*
> *and recovery of sight for the blind, to set the*
> *oppressed free, to proclaim the year of the*
> *Lord's favor. Then he rolled up the scroll, gave*
> *it back to the attendant and sat down. The*
> *eyes of everyone in the synagogue were*
> *fastened on him. He began by saying to them,*
> *"Today this scripture is fulfilled in your*
> *hearing."(Luke 4:16-21, NIV)*

Like us, Jesus cycled through this pattern more than once during His life. The pattern can be seen again when Jesus allowed Himself to be captured and bound by the High Priest's guards and submitted Himself to the Roman torture and the cross. Those hours were another type of willing bondage, an Egypt, Jesus went through. Jesus left that Egypt at the same moment He left the Egypt of His natural body, when He gave up His Spirit and died. At death, He began another wilderness crossing that included the testing and pain of being separated from the Father. He arrived at hell's gate, but it found no ability to hold Him. As He said while alive, the Devil could find nothing in Him. Because death could not hold Him, He took its authority away over mankind. Once again, Jesus came out of the wilderness crossing of death stronger in the spirit with resurrection power! Rising victorious, He began claiming more portions of His inheritance, as Captain of our Salvation, the

First Fruit from the dead, and King of the earth. Jesus is such a boss!

Chapter 2 – Questions

1. When you received salvation, what were some immediate ways that you saw yourself coming out of a type of Egypt?

2. Have you ever walked through a wilderness crossing season of life that you can confidently look back on and see an area where your trust in God deepened? What were you able to do afterwards that you couldn't do before?

3. Describe in your words what you think a season of claiming inheritance would look like for you personally.

SESSION 2 – VIDEO QUESTIONS

1. Can you share a time when you needed a spiritual breakthrough from an unhealthy cycle and how you broke out of it?

2. If you find yourself in a wilderness of wandering season, what do you think is something you can do, to move out of that place into another season?

Chapter 3 – Two Sides of A Coin

If you thought there was a place missing from where the children of Israel traveled in the last chapter, there was. Though God delivered them from Egypt, brought them through the wilderness crossing, and then to the edge of their inheritance, they refused to enter in fear of the giants in the land. Because of their disobedience, God turned the whole congregation back around to wander in the wilderness for about forty years. This second wilderness experience carries with it a different spiritual meaning for us than their first.

The first wilderness crossing is part of a healthy maturing cycle for believers, the second trip into the wilderness is not. The children of Israel went through the first wilderness crossing because of obedience, their second trip into the wilderness was because of disobedience. There is a difference between walking through hard times because you're following God, and walking through hard times because you're not! If you're like me, you've probably experienced both in your life.

On their first walk through the wilderness, the children of Israel were on their way somewhere, to their inheritance. On their second trip into the wilderness, they were literally going nowhere! The wilderness of wandering represents to us exactly what it was to the children of Israel, a place of roaming, lost dreams, and restlessness. The wilderness of wandering is a place with no sense of purpose or fulfillment. It's a place with no dominion, and no authority. The wilderness of wandering, isn't meant for thriving, it's meant for dying!

At the age of thirty, I began to see a pattern in my life. Because I was pursuing the Lord, He would consistently set me free from strongholds in my mind, or types of Egypt. During those times, I had many opportunities to see if the freedom He gave me really had become a part of my walk. I would come to a precipice, feeling that my walk with the Lord and the fruit of it should enter into a new place. Instead of moving on, I kept falling backwards only to wonder where the promises were.

It was while reading the children of Israel's story and seeing this pattern in their walk from Egypt to their inheritance that I realized the exact same thing was happening to me! God was bringing me to the edge of my inheritance expecting me to claim the promises, but each time I was shrinking back at the taunting of my giant, the spirit of fear. When the Lord began to reveal to me the goodness, waiting for me in my inheritance on the other side of that giant, I got mad, really mad! I began to hate the dumpy wilderness of wandering I had been in for so long! I wanted my inheritance!

Right in the middle of that season of beginning to see my inheritance God brought me just the revelation I needed to more fully understand how my actions (or inactions) were holding me back from the promise of my inheritance. I was taking a theology class on the life of David when my professor, Doctor Ron Cottle, began expounding on the two Hebrew words that mean inherit, nachal and yarash. Their meanings and the subtle difference between the two words, were two sides of the same coin I needed to see to move forward.

The two Hebrew words nachal and yarash aren't little side notes in scripture that you have to dig around in some obscure passages to find. In fact, the Hebrew words for inheritance and their forms are used over five hundred times in the Old Testament. That is about three hundred more times than the word salvation, four hundred more times than forgive, three hundred more times than the word grace, and three hundred more times than the word, worship! Once you are aware of this theme of inheritance, you see it everywhere you look in the scripture.

NACHALAH

The Hebrew word nachalah and its shortened form nachal are mostly translated heritage, inherit, and possession. Nachalah means to get as a possession or to acquire. It is used to define a specific portion or share of something, usually land. The shortened form, nachal, means to bequeath, distribute, or to leave for a certain person or persons. Usually when nachal is used it's to describe an inheritance based on whose child you are, or whose family you are in. It carries with it, the idea of sonship.

When Moses was giving instructions as to how the land of Canaan should be divided, he said it would be divided according to tribes and then the families within the tribes. In other words, each tribe would get a large piece of land, then within that larger tract, the individual inheritances would be given out to the families from that tribe only.

> *"But the land shall be divided by lot. They shall receive **their inheritance (nachal)** according to the names of the tribes of their fathers. (Num. 26:55, NAS)*

Who your parents are makes a big difference in your life, wouldn't you agree? Since we are God's children, we are entitled to certain rights and privileges. One of those is our nachal, inheritance. When it comes to your inheritance, from God, being entitled is a good thing!

> *"The Spirit Himself bears witness with our spirit that we are children of God. And if children, then heirs--heirs of God and joint heirs with Christ, if indeed we suffer with Him, that we may also be glorified together."* (Rom. 8:16-17, NKJV)

On at least one occasion, Moses asked God to have mercy on the children of Israel, for no other reason than that they were Abraham's children. While the children of Israel sat at the foot of Mt. Sinai, Moses went up to the mountain to receive the law from God. On one of his trips, he was gone so long the people began to question if he was ever coming back. Instead of waiting for instructions from God through Moses, they decided to make their own god. The people threw their gold into a fire, melted it down and created a golden calf. They began to make sacrifices to it and declare, *"This is the god who brought us out of Egypt!" (Exodus 32:4, Paraphrased)*

God saw what the people were doing and told Moses to get down from the mountain. He was so mad that He told Moses, stand back, I'm going to wipe them out and make another nation out of you. It's actually a funny interchange between God and Moses when you read it. God starts off furious, and Moses seems to calm Him down. Once God relents, it's Moses's turn to let the people have it! He came off that mountain so angry that he threw down the original ten commandments, breaking them in pieces. But before Moses's outburst, he had the cool head to ask God to forgive the people. Moses reminded God with one word that it was the legal right of the children of Israel to have the opportunity to move forward and possess the land.

> *"...Turn from Your fierce wrath, and relent from this harm to Your people. Remember Abraham, Isaac, and Israel, your servants to whom You swore by Your own self, and said to them, I will multiply your descendants as the stars of heaven; and all this land that I have spoken* **of I give to your descendants, and they shall inherit (nachal) it forever.** *So the Lord relented from the harm which He said He would do to His people."*
> *(Ex. 32:12-14, NKJV)*

45

Jesus told Nicodemus, no one can see the Kingdom of God unless they are born again. Jesus used that term for a very specific reason. Quite literally at the moment of our conversion we are born into God's family and the right of a nachal inheritance becomes ours. As God's son or daughter, He has promised you an inheritance in His Kingdom. This is why when Jesus met Paul on the road to Damascus, He said tell them about the forgiveness of sin and their inheritance. Bringing us into God's family through the forgiveness of sin enables us to have the inheritance God longs to share with us.

> *And because ye are sons, God hath sent*
> *forth the Spirit of his Son into your hearts,*
> *crying, Abba, Father. Wherefore thou art no*
> *more a servant, but a son; and if a son, then*
> *an heir of God through Christ.*
> *(Gal. 4:6-7, KJV)*

We are God's children and He is our Father. This is a simple statement, but if you really think about what that statement means, it should blow your mind! The Creator of the universe calls you child. The one who formed the galaxies, and everything that is in them, has an eternal Kingdom and He wants to share it with you!

If you grew up with parents who gave you good things, loved you, and encouraged you, it's easy to see God as good with a great inheritance to share with you. If you grew up with parents that weren't trustworthy, discouraged you, or brought pain into your life, that is how you will tend to see God. No matter which side of the pendulum you find yourself on, there is no doubt our human parents and the circumstances of our upbringing greatly shape how we see God and our belief that He has good things for us. It was the same for the children of Israel.

The generation that God led out of Egypt grew up in slavery, under the influence of the Egyptian gods who were capricious in nature. The wilderness crossing was meant to help them see themselves as God's children and Him as a good Father, so that when the time came, they would claim their inheritance. Sadly, they never changed their minds about God or themselves. They didn't believe He would really give them the inheritance He promised. That first generation never received the inheritance even though it was rightly theirs.

It's no different for us today. If we don't believe that God has good things for us, will we experience them? The good news is God is willing to spend our lives convincing us of our sonship and of His goodness if He needs to.....OR we can choose to believe He has good things for us just because we are His children.

YARASH

While nachalah is the portion of our inheritance, that just naturally flows to you because of whose child you are, yarash is usually used to show action, something that is sought after in some way. Look how yarash is used in the following scriptures:

Speaking to Abraham God said:

> *I will certainly bless you. I will multiply your descendants beyond number, like the stars in the sky and the sand on the seashore. Your descendants **will conquer (yarash) the cities of their enemies.***
> *(Gen. 22:17, NLT)*

The enemies of Israel said this about them:

> *The enemy boasted, 'I will chase them and catch up with them. I will plunder them and consume them. I will flash my sword; **my powerful hand will destroy (yarash) them.***
> *(Ex. 15:9, NLT)*

47

God told Israel this is what He would do when they came to their inheritance:

> ***I will drive out (yarash) the other nations***
> ***ahead*** *of you and expand your territory, so no*
> *one will covet and conquer your land while*
> *you appear before the LORD your God three*
> *times each year. (Ex. 34:24, NLT)*

You can see the intensity of the word yarash. Not only is it translated conquer, destroy, and drive out, it's also translated, to possess, to dispossess, to take possession of, inherit, disinherit, occupy and heir. Strong's says its main meaning is to **occupy by driving out previous tenants** and possessing in their place. This is exactly what God was asking the children of Israel to do when He brought them up to the edge of their inheritance in the land of Canaan.

Yarash is the other side of the inheritance coin that I needed to see as I stood on the shores of the Jordan in that season. During that time, I finally came to terms with the fact that all the things God had for me in this life weren't just going to fall into my lap. No. I needed to start taking, forward moving, steps of faith that would include facing the giant of the spirit of fear, that had held me at bay for so long. This was the realization I needed to lay hold of, there was going to be a fight!

Just like the children of Israel, there will be parts of our inheritance that we will have to conquer and occupy by driving someone else out! Their giants were in the natural, ours are in the spiritual. Because we live in a fallen world, there will be things and places in this life that God meant for us to have, that the enemy tries to prevent us from walking in. Just like the enemy filled the children of Israel's inheritance with giants, he has tried to fill ours with giants as well. These giants can be in the form of generational sins, strongholds in our minds, and circumstances outside of ourselves. These are the parts of our inheritance that we will have to yarash.

Learning about this Hebrew word yarash and what it means, has been so life changing for me, because, I like many other Christians had fallen into this false belief that everything God wanted for me, would just fall into my lap. I'm afraid, we have taken the message of grace(which is good) and used it to justify our complacency when it comes to our relationship with the Lord. We start saying things like " If God wants me to have it He will work it out." While that is true in a sense, we also sometimes have to drive out, or dispossess something in the spirit that is standing in the way of " What God has for us." As people who desire to be mature, learning to ask these questions and knowing the action to take if the answer is yes, something is standing in your way, are key to our walking in the fullness God intends for us to in this life.

THERE IS A DIFFERENCE

Nachal is what is automatically yours because of whose family you belong to, while yarash is the part of your inheritance you have to get up and pursue. The nachal portion of your inheritance is linked to your **identity** as God's child, the yarash portion is linked to the **actions** you take based on that belief.

Many believers aren't secure in their identity which stops them from moving forward in the things God has called them to. Think about the difference and the connection between the two sides of your whole inheritance from this simple illustration. When a child enters their parents' home, whether they are five years old or forty-five, they will freely open the refrigerator and grab out whatever they want to eat or drink. They will simply take it. Why? Because as the child of their parents they know whatever is in that refrigerator is available to them. Now if that same person were in someone else's home, they would not go into their refrigerator without asking permission simply because they are not that person's child.

Unfortunately, too many Christians don't feel at home with God. They feel like visitors who are unworthy to open the refrigerator in His house. They know in their head, they are God's child, but still doubt in their heart. They aren't sure if there is a place for them in His house. The ability to walk in the fullness of both the nachal and yarash portions of your inheritance are related to one another, they are two sides of one coin.

Nachal says you have authority because you are God's child. Yarash is the action you take based on that belief. The difference between those who will yarash and those who won't, is how they see themselves, their identity.

Our identities have become such a complex topic, worthy of the many books and sermons that have addressed it. But in the abundance of information and opinions, I've found it most helpful to go back to the simplicity of our identity found in the garden of Eden. Adam was made in the image of God the way a son or daughter is made in the image of their parents. He was to tend and keep the garden, or you could say, Adam was to yarash, or stand in possession of it. Adam didn't have to take it out of anyone's hands, but he was to actively keep it out of someone's hands, which he did not do.

All of Adam's work and ability to yarash flowed from the identity God gave to him as His son. As a son, Adam was to be completely dependent on God for his ability to do what God called him to do. This is the original state of man, that Jesus came to give back to us. His desire is for us to lean into an intimate relationship with God in order to accomplish that which He created us for. Just like God breathed His life into Adam, giving him his identity, God also wants to breathe identity into us. We will never yarash our inheritance beyond what we believe we possess from the place of our nachal, or understanding that we are fully God's children.

Adam chose self-reliance over dependence on God. If we want to know how deep the roots of our identity are in God, we must ask ourselves, how much do I depend on Him? Do I live a life with my hands, and my heart wide open knowing He has got me, or do tightly grip everything, depending on myself and others more than God? So let me ask you, how much do you rely on God for your money, job, kids, marriage? What does that look like? Does it mean we do nothing? No, it means we do everything that God asks us to do, all the while knowing we don't control any of it. We follow His spirit and let the outcome be His. Though He has called us to do great and mighty things in this life, it all flows from a place of depending on Him as a little child depends upon their parents. This is freedom, this is walking in both side of your inheritance, nachal and yarash.

KNOW YOUR SEASON!

Not only do nachal and yarash represent sonship and the works we do based on that belief, these two words also represent seasons in your life. There was a season for the children of Israel to discover their identity (nachal) as God's special people, and there was a season for them to take action (yarash) based on that belief. It doesn't matter how long you have walked with God, there will be seasons God will take you through to focus you in on your identity in Him (nachal), and out of those times will come seasons of climbing the next mountain placed in front of you (yarashing). Every time your identity gets more rooted in God, you can climb a little higher up the mountains before you. Some have learned to go in and out of these seasons so well and for so long, that they are no longer just defeating their own giants, and climbing their own mountains, they are helping others do the same. We call these people spiritual giants.

The first time I taught on this theme of our inheritance in Jesus, I was working at a local house of prayer in Burlington, Vermont. It was a small ministry, so many of us were serving

51

in multiple positions. I was heading up the children's ministry and coordinating Bible teachings for the community. At that time, my family and I were living in a little town called Jericho which sat in the valley of Mt. Mansfield. Our home was situated across from a farmer's field with an unobstructed view of the mountain.

While spending time with the Lord on a cold February morning, God whispered the phrase to me "Free hearts." At the time, I believed it was an invitation to partner with Him in what He longs to do, set people free. The following summer when I was in the middle of doing the inheritance teachings for the first time, at the house of prayer, the Lord reminded me of the phrase, free hearts. At that time, He started making it clear not only to me, but my sister-in-law Susan as well, that "Free hearts" was more than a phrase, it was the name of a ministry He was birthing in us as we were ministering, this truth that we have an inheritance in Him.

At God's prompting we launched Free Hearts, diving in head first. We told everyone that would listen that the Lord wanted us to start a Bible teaching ministry called Free Hearts. We started getting together with some friends to pray over this amazing invitation. One day the Lord spoke to us that we were to be a portable ministry. We began going from house to house, teaching the word and ministering to women. Those meetings were so sweet and impactful not only for all who came, but for us as well.

In what seemed like no time at all, Susan and I, two homeschooling moms each suddenly had become good at marketing, making videos, databases, and a whole lot of other stuff it takes to run a ministry. When we began doing day long events, we recruited our husbands, kids, and many sweet friends who were willing to help out. It was all for the Lord and we loved it! In those early days we were ready to yarash any mountain and slay any giant we thought was in our way!

Around two years into the ministry, a problem came, at least for me. I suddenly felt as if I had no vision, no direction, and had no new teachings. I went through a couple months feeling all spiritually dried up inside. I tried avoiding doing any ministry for those months, but I also desperately didn't want to lose the momentum we were experiencing. I called a special prayer meeting with all the ladies who had become an integral part of our ministry over the last two years. We scheduled it for a Saturday morning at a friend's big farm house in the mountains. We were primarily going to worship, have a time of corporate prayer, and then enjoy lunch together. I was relieved that I didn't feel the need to do a teaching as I felt I had nothing to offer, however I knew that the ladies who had supported us were looking to me to share the direction we saw the ministry going. Since I wasn't sure where we were going, that was going to be kinda hard to do!

I woke up early the morning of our prayer gathering totally discouraged. I was the leader, but what was I going to share? I desperately sought the Lord for a word, a direction, a mountain to climb, something to yarash! Then the Lord gently pointed me to this scripture:

> *Who is among you that feareth the LORD,*
> *that obeyeth the voice of his servant, that*
> *walketh in darkness, and hath no light? let*
> *him trust in the name of the LORD, and stay*
> *upon his God. Behold, all ye that kindle a fire,*
> *that compass yourselves about with sparks:*
> *walk in the light of your fire, and in the*
> *sparks that ye have kindled. This shall ye*
> *have of mine hand; ye shall lie down in*
> *sorrow. (Isa. 50:11-12, KJV)*

I felt the Holy Spirit drawing me into these scriptures and for the next few minutes, they became my dialogue with the Lord.

Who among you fears Yahweh?

"I fear you Lord." I responded.
Who obeys the voice of His Servant, Jesus?

"I obey you Lord." With my lip quivering.

Who walks in darkness and has no light?

"Me!" I cried, "I am in the dark!"

Let him trust in the name of the LORD and stay upon His God.

God had the final word, and it was the answer I needed. "Let
him trust in the name of the LORD and stay upon His God." As
I read that verse, it washed over me like a gentle wave. God
had me in the dark on purpose! My vision was clouded because
He wanted it to be! In that moment of enjoying the peace of His
presence, He whispered, "What is the other word that means to
inherit?" I knew in my spirit what He meant for the "other
word." Immediately, I responded, "nachal." The revelation
entered my spirit, my Heavenly Father wanted me to sit in the
dark, so that I could remember who I am. There was no
mountain to climb and no giant to slay in that season. It was a
season not to go and do, but to receive. I was no longer in a
season of yarashing, it was a season of identity, of nachal.
Before that moment, I didn't even realize these two words also
represented two different seasons of life, but they do. The next
few months were a time of firming up my foundations and
receiving a deeper revelation of my identity as His beloved
daughter.

I went to the prayer meeting and shared my conversation
with God that morning. With a heart full of thanksgiving that
God leads us so well, I shared as a ministry we were entering a
new season of waiting and receiving. We weren't going to
"kindle our own fires" as it were, coming up with the next great

idea, we were going to wait on God. A couple ladies who were there that morning later told me that while I was sharing, they felt the Holy Spirit convicting them in different areas of their lives where they had been trying to "kindle their own fires." They too needed a change of mind, a change of season.

My lesson was obvious, know your seasons. We all must go in and out of these two seasons, nachal and yarash. We can't get it twisted as my pastor often says, the more mountains He lets us climb the more giants we face, the easier it would become to start thinking we are the one doing it. We must always remember it's God doing the work in and through us. We can do nothing apart from our identity being firmly rooted in Him.

We can never earn God's love, our salvation, the forgiveness of sins, or eternal life. They are all part of our nachal, inheritance. But please remember, as I prod you on in this journey to yarash your inheritance that everything we ever "do" or yarash is out of the abundance of God's grace that He has freely given us. It's His grace that empowers us to do. Every lasting work that we will ever do originates from God, is for God, and is by God.

The following spring after that revelation of my need to rest in the nachal, part of my inheritance, God did so much more with Free Hearts than we could have ever dreamed or imagined. I have found that when you're in a season of nachal, it's a season of preparation.

Learning the difference between these two words for our inheritance has personally helped me make sense of so much of my own walk with the Lord. It's from the understanding of these two words, coupled with the fact that the land of Israel represents our inheritance, that I have been able to see and walk in so much more of what God has for me. Anytime I feel like I'm lost or I don't know what's going on in my spiritual walk, I go back to the cycles I showed you in the last chapter and say, "Where am I here God?" Then I go back to these two words and ask which season am I in. It has helped me so much and I hope it helps you too!

Chapter 3 – Questions

1. What do you think about these two words (nachal and yarash) that both mean to inherit but have very different meanings?

2. Why do you think there are things in this life that God wants us to have that don't just fall into our laps?

3. Why does understanding our identity and walking in our nachal inheritance, need to come before we can go after our yarash portion of inheritance, or our destiny?

SESSION 3 – VIDEO QUESTIONS

1. If you took away all comparisons and expectations, what you would begin pursuing?

2. Which season do you find yourself more naturally drawn to, seasons of rest, or seasons of action?

3. Which season are you currently in, nachal or yarash?

Chapter 4 – Preparation is Key

In 2010, the Nashville area experienced major flooding that made national news. The flood devastated much of the area, including the neighborhood behind mine. At least 5 homes were completely destroyed to the point they were condemned and torn down. Being an older neighborhood, it didn't have an underground system to deal with excessive water. After the flood, the city installed cement stormwater canals in the neighborhood to help carry water away from the homes should another flood come.

My husband, Chris, and I frequently went on walks through the neighborhood behind ours that was hit so hard by the flood. Besides talking with Chris while we walked, I also enjoyed looking at the uniqueness and beauty of the homes. As we went on our walks, I noticed one of the newly installed water canals was placed in between two homes. While one property owner may think it's great to have the water canal there because it gives the water a place to go, another person may see it as an invitation for water to run towards your property.

During our walks, I noticed one of the property owners beside the water canal was periodically having large piles of dirt delivered and dumped close to the storm canal. After the dirt was delivered, he systematically spread it by hand over the edge of his yard, closest to the canal. He then planted grass seed, and repeated the process again a few months later. After about a year and a half he managed to build up the edge of his yard so that it was significantly higher than his neighbor's on the other side. All this labor intensive work was being done by a man I estimate to be in his seventies! As I watched over time, I knew what he was doing, he was preparing for the next flood. When storm waters come again, his property will be much

59

harder to reach now being about four feet higher than his neighbors.

The point of preparation is to be ready when the suddenlies of life come. Floods come suddenly, but oftentimes so do opportunities. God knew there would be a day when the children of Israel would be brought up to the edge of their inheritance and He wanted them ready to yarash it when that day came. In our fast paced, instant gratification world the art and necessity of preparation often gets overlooked. But preparation is not lost on God.

John the Baptist's whole ministry was to prepare the people of Israel for the coming of the Messiah. David spent most of his life amassing great wealth, preparing to have what was needed to build the temple for God. Even Jesus knows what it means to prepare.

> *"In my Father's house are many mansions:*
> *if it were not so, I would have told you. I go to*
> *prepare a place for you. And if I go and*
> *prepare a place for you, I will come again, and*
> *receive you unto myself; that where I am,*
> *there ye may be also."*
> *(John 14:2-3, KJV)*

When we experience a missed opportunity in life, often it's because we missed more than just a moment. Many times what we missed was the preparation needed to seize the moment, when the opportunity comes. Though God had done all He could to prepare the children of Israel to claim their inheritance, during the wilderness crossing they faltered when the opportunity to yarash or seize the land was at hand. They didn't let the wilderness crossing do it's intended work of preparation.

After God called our family to move to Tennessee we began saying our good-byes to all the communities we were a part of. I vividly remember the last Sunday service we attended at our home church. Right as I was about to leave, a lady I only knew casually came up to me and handed me a small piece of paper. She told me as she was showering that morning the Lord began to talk to her about me. She said she had to jump out of the shower and grab a piece of paper so she could quickly write it down.

After reading it, I knew beyond a shadow of a doubt that the word was from God. She wrote several phrases God often said to me through the years, things that only I knew. That piece of paper has been in my Bible the last three years. I read it at least once a week because it talks about my future. The first three phrases written on this powerful message to me are, be prepared, be prepared, be prepared!

Preparation is key when it comes to claiming your inheritance. Preparation is the overarching theme of the wilderness crossing seasons of life. I couldn't have known when she gave me that note, how correct it was. I can only look back now and tell you, the last three years of my life have been full of tests and trials, all meant to prepare me for the season of inheritance I'm stepping into. And just like the children of Israel, I've had lessons to learn in the wilderness crossing I've found myself in. Remembering the Apostle Paul's warning in Corinthians, that their journey was written for us I want to highlight three areas every believer needs to pay attention to when it comes to preparing for a season of inheritance through a wilderness crossing.

1-THEIR WORDS

Three days after the children of Israel left Egypt, the full force of the Egyptian army came after them with the intent to drag them back to Egypt. God made a way of escape for them by parting the Red Sea, but not before the children of Israel said:

> *"Because there were no graves in Egypt,*
> *have you taken us away to die in the*
> *wilderness? Why have you so dealt with us, to*
> *bring us up out of Egypt?" (Ex. 14:11, NKJV)*

After this, they followed God's presence in the cloud by day and fire by night, going deeper into the wilderness. Approximately 6 weeks after their exodus from Egypt, they ran out of food. God miraculously sent them food they called manna, but not before they said:

> *"Oh that we had died by the hand of the*
> *LORD in the land of Egypt, when we sat by*
> *the pots of meat and when we ate bread to the*
> *full! For you have brought us out into this*
> *wilderness to kill this whole assembly with*
> *hunger."*
> *(Ex. 16:3, NKJV)*

They continued their journey and no matter how many times they moved, the manna showed up six days a week for them to gather, prepare, and eat. Soon after the provision of manna, they ran out of water again. At that time, God miraculously provided water from a rock, after they said :

> *And the people thirsted there for water,*
> *and the people complained against Moses, and*
> *said, "Why is it you have brought us up out of*
> *Egypt, to kill us and our children and our*
> *livestock with thirst?"*
> *(Ex. 17:3, NKJV)*

After their approximately two year trek through the wilderness they arrived at the edge of their inheritance at reports of giants in the land, they said:

> *"If only we had died in the land of Egypt!*
> *Or if only we had died in this wilderness! Why*
> *has the LORD brought us to this land to fall by*
> *the sword, that our wives and children should*

become victims? Would it not be better for us
to return to Egypt?" (Num. 14:2-3, NKJV)

At each trial God was not only looking at what they were doing, He was also listening to what they were saying.

Now when the people complained, it
displeased the Lord; for the Lord heard it...
(Num. 11:1, NKJV)

When I read these passages, I don't throw stones at the children of Israel. I have never traveled through the wilderness with my entire family and all my possessions while having to depend on God's supernatural provision for food, water, or deliverance from an enemy chasing me. But I have been following God only to come upon some troubles, needs, and difficult situations. What I have learned from the children of Israel is this, no matter what my circumstances, I need to be careful what I say.

WE WERE CREATED IN HIS IMAGE

God created us in His image. When God wanted to create the worlds and everything that we understand to exist, He spoke. While we don't have the power to create galaxies and planets, our words do have power!

Death and life are in the power of the
tongue, and those who love it will eat its fruit.
(Prov. 18:21, NKJV)

In the scripture God's word is said to be like a seed. *(Matt. 13)* The wonder of seeds are that contained within them is an embryo, or the plant itself in baby form. When the seed begins to grow, one part of the embryo becomes the plant while the other part becomes the root. In other words the essence of the fully manifest pant is held within the tiny seed. If the seed is planted, watered, and encouraged to grow, what will grow is what was in the seed, not something different. Because we are made in the image of God, every word we speak is like a little seed as well. If it finds a heart or circumstance to land in, and water to make it grow, what is contained in the seed, is what will manifest. This is what the verse in Proverbs means, we can speak seeds that contain death, or seeds that contain life. The children of Israel, sowed words of death in the wilderness over themselves consistently and that is exactly what they ate.

> *"How long shall I bear with this evil congregation who complain against Me? I have heard the complaints which the children of Israel make against Me. Say to them, As I live, says the **LORD, just as you have spoken in My hearing, so I will do to you: The carcasses of you who have complained against Me shall fall in this wilderness..."***
> *(Num. 14:27-29, NKJV)*

When situations get hard, we don't have to say exactly how we think or want them to turn out, we only need to align our words with WHO God is. When God told Moses His name, He said, I am who I am. That means, God is all in all. God is everything good and wonderful that we need Him to be at any point in life. God is a friend to the lonely, a comforter to the hurting, and merciful to those who cry out for mercy. God is a parent to the orphan, and a spouse to the widow, and healer to the sick. If we plant the seed of God's character over a situation, and continue to water and nurture it, God's character is what will grow in that circumstance. There is so much power in aligning our words with who God is by declaring His character over every situation!

Do you know that God really does listen to your words? At every turn, God was listening to the children of Israel to see if they would align their words with the truth of who He is. When they had no food or water in the wilderness, they should have said, "God will provide for us as He has already done." When

64

they heard of giants in the land, the whole congregation should have said, "God defeated the Egyptians, and the Amalekites, He will give us this victory as well." I want to challenge you when tough times arise, to open your mouth and begin to declare God's character over that situation.

Even if you are having a hard time believing what you are saying, I believe that as you declare the truth of who God is, the words of truth will quicken, which means to stimulate or to make come alive, your spirit. In other words, at the sound of the truth of who God is, your spirit, your mind, and your emotions will begin to align with truth, and you will believe. Don't wait until you feel it to say it, say it to help yourself begin to feel it!

As we move through this life, we have the ability to plant seeds of life or death over ourselves, others, and our circumstances with our words. What we repeatedly say will have an effect on us like it did the children of Israel. Many believers I feel are not walking in their inheritance, because they have cursed themselves over and over again. If this is you, I encourage you to take the next season and begin to ask God to bring back to your remembrance all the bad seeds you have sown with your words. Then dig them up through confession and repentance, and in their place, plant words full of the power and life of God!

2 – ARE YOU LOOKING FORWARDS OR BACKWARDS?

You may be surprised to see that subtitle. Looking back isn't something we usually think of as a big sin, and I don't think it is, but always looking back can be a stumbling block to possessing your inheritance.

God isn't in time, but He put us in time, and time is moving forward not backward. A good friend of mine, Pastor Brad

Keller made this point once while preaching: "When you are driving your car, you are going somewhere, there is a destination in mind. To get to where you are going you look through a large window in front of you. To keep us safe on the road we do from time to time need to look and see what is behind us, yet we only have a little mirror to look back." The journey of life should be seen like driving a car. The view and focus ahead should be larger than what's behind. Once Jesus asked a man to follow Him, and the man said yes, but first let me go back and bury my father. Another man, told Jesus he would follow Him too, but before he could begin, he needed to go back and say good-bye to his family. Jesus responded to them; *No one, having put his hand to the plow, and looking back, is fit for the Kingdom of God." (Luke 9:62, NKJV)*

In the Kingdom of God, there is a pull forward, an urgency to move ahead. Almost every time the children of Israel complained about their circumstances in the wilderness, they referenced their past in Egypt. Oh, the meat we had in Egypt, oh, the leeks we had in Egypt, they said. They kept, seeing themselves, back in Egypt, not the place ahead of them, their inheritance!

This is one of the dangers of looking back, we can tend to romanticize the past if we look too long. To listen to the children of Israel talk, it was like they completely forgot all the horrible things that happened to them in Egypt. Hello, the Egyptians were killing their baby boys when they escaped! Why would they have ever talked about Egypt as a good place, except that they had begun romanticizing it?

Eventually, like any fantasy we let go on too long, looking back can ensnare our minds so that we can't move forward, and that's exactly what it did to the children of Israel. When they were given the chance to enter their inheritance, they turned around in their minds and wanted to go back to Egypt! They were exactly where Satan wanted them all along, stuck in the past.

In the New Testament, a man named Stephen stood before the Jewish counsel to share with them the good news about Jesus. He began with an eloquent summary of the nation of Israel's history. As he spoke, Stephen pointed them back to this generation who refused to move forward into their inheritance. He said, *"whom our fathers would not obey, but rejected. And in their hearts they turned back to Egypt"* (Acts 7:39, NKJV)

Stephen was in emphasizing this point as he was addressing the leaders of the nation, because they were doing the same thing in Stephen's day. Instead of moving forward and claiming the truth of the nation's inheritance that Jesus is the Messiah, they were choosing to remain in captivity to Rome, because that is what they knew. Being captive to what we've known by keeping our eyes focused there will cause us to miss the portion of inheritance that is in front of us.

While we should learn from our mistakes and understand why we are the way we are because of our past we cannot remain there in our minds. Remembering the past is different from staying stuck there. Our lives are a forward moving journey into the things of God. Jesus said follow Me, because He has somewhere to take us on this journey called life.

Twice in my life God has asked me to move. In order to move to a new and unknown place, both times I had to cling to this truth, don't look back! I grew up in a rural county in Virginia. Most of my dad's side and many of my mom's side of my family lived fairly close by. There was something so comforting to me to know so much of my family was near.

When the time came for Chris and I to get our first home, we were able to buy four acres right next to my parents. We built our home not only beside my parents but also beside my sister's and older brother's homes. People always joked and said we lived in a compound. There were ten acres and eight kids between my siblings and I. But hey, we were one big happy family, and we enjoyed living next to each other.

When we built our house we never planned to move, so we built our dream home. It was a raised ranch so it really ended up being like two houses in one. On the upper level we had our main living area, bedrooms, and a sunroom. On the lower level we put in a hair salon for me to be able to work from home. The lower level also included an extra kitchen, a weight room, an office, another living room, and a game room with a pool table. All this went out to our back deck and huge inground pool. We were truly living large!

Not only did we love our home, but we enjoyed the many benefits of having family so near. The biggest being that my mom homeschooled all my kids, with my sister's help. All my children had to do each day was walk next door to Mammaw's house where she had an amazing school room set up just for them, not to mention she was a great teacher. Life was good! Needless to say, when we moved from a place where I felt like I had everything, to a place where I felt like I had nothing is when I had to learn the lesson to not look back.

The first year in Vermont, I cried, and I cried. I left so much behind. I had spent all of my life in Virginia, yet now I lived in Vermont! I had to fight to constantly refocus life in front of me. The only thing that kept me moving forward was the dramatic and undeniable way in which God spoke to us to move. I knew in my heart that going back would be disobedience. More than an easy life, I wanted what God had for me. During that season, I had to train my mind to look forward and not back. I learned how to declare the goodness of God over my life and my family, even when I didn't see it. At the time of these battles to keep my eyes ahead, I had no idea the good things God had in store for our family in Vermont. It's only now having walked through eight years there that I can look back and see the wonderful plan God had all along. All which I would have missed had I allowed myself to stay stuck in the past.

After eight years in Vermont, God called our family to Tennessee and I've had to do the same thing all over again. Turned out, the life God built for us in Vermont had become a really great one too. It was hard to leave and think about starting all over again. It was right as God asked us to leave that so many doors were opening for our ministry, Free Hearts. We've been in Tennessee for three years now and I've had to apply the same principles of staying forward focused. I don't know what is ahead, all I know is God said, and so I believe.

> *Blessed is the man whose strength is in*
> *You, whose heart is set on pilgrimage.*
> *(Psalm 84:5, NKJV)*

Whether your past was good or bad, you can't stay stuck there! The way of life winds upward for the wise. The best is yet to come!

3 – ARE WE HONORING?

I can't help but think that from the children of Israel's point of view, God's appointment of Moses as their leader may not have been very welcomed. After all, Moses didn't grow up like them as a slave in Egypt. Quite the opposite, Moses spent the first forty years of his life as the adopted son of Pharaoh's daughter. If that's not enough of a contrast, after he was exiled from Egypt for killing an Egyptian, he spent the next forty years with his family living in the land of Midian as a free man. I can easily see how many of the leaders of the children of Israel would have resisted his leadership.

Even Moses doubted how they would receive him, when God spoke to him from the burning bush, he said:

> *"Who am I that I should go to Pharaoh, and*
> *that I should bring the children of Israel out of*
> *Egypt?" (Ex. 3:11, NKJV)*

It didn't matter that Moses felt unqualified, and it didn't matter if the people thought he was unqualified. God called him to lead the people out of slavery to their inheritance, and as God's appointed leader, the people were to honor him.

The Hebrew word we translate into honor is kabad. Kabad means to be heavy or weighty. If something is heavy or weighty, it also naturally must take up space. I think of honoring someone as giving them a space in my heart that is equal to the position God has given them.

In the case of Moses, since he was the God appointed spiritual leader of the entire congregation of Israel, he should have had much honor, or great space in the hearts of the people. But that was not always the case, in fact, Moses' own sister and brother dishonored him. At Moses' marriage to an Ethiopian woman, Miriam and Aaron question that decision, which lead them to start questioning him all together.

> "Has the LORD indeed spoken only
> through Moses? Has He not spoken through
> us also?" And the LORD heard it.
> (Num. 12:2, NKJV)

God wasn't too happy with their apparent lack of honor towards Moses, His appointed leader, so God came and told them about themselves:

> Then the LORD came down in a pillar of
> cloud; he stood at the entrance to the tent and
> summoned Aaron and Miriam. When the two
> of them stepped forward, ⁶he said, "Listen to
> my words: "When there is a prophet among
> you, I, the LORD, reveal myself to them in
> visions, I speak to them in dreams. But this is
> not true of my servant Moses; he is faithful in
> all my house.ˢ With him I speak face to face;
> clearly and not in riddles; he sees the form of

the LORD. Why then were you not afraid to
speak against my servant Moses?"
(Num. 12: 5-8, NIV)

God said they should have been afraid to speak against Moses. After the presence of God left, Miriam was full of leprosy and was forced to stay outside the camp. Moses interceded for her, and after a week she was healed and brought back into the community.

After his own brother and sister dishonored him, another group decided to do the same thing. Dishonor is like a weed easily grown once planted it can affect whole groups. This second example took place after they missed their chance to enter their inheritance, but I can't help but to think after all their complaining, this was typical of how the people treated Moses.

Two hundred and fifty leaders of Israel rose up to speak against Moses. Their claim was he shouldn't be the ones giving orders. Specifically these men questioned why only the Levites could do the priestly duties, they thought anyone should be able to serve in the tabernacle of the Lord. Moses said if you want to, go ahead. God will show you who He appointed and who He hasn't. Moses said;

"By this you shall know that the LORD has
sent me to do all these works, for I have not
done them of my own will. If these men die
naturally like all men, or if they are visited by
the common fate of all men, then the LORD
has not sent me. But if the LORD creates a
new thing, and the earth opens its mouth and
swallows them up with all that belongs to
them, and they go down alive into the pit,
then you will understand that these men have
rejected the LORD." (Num. 16: 28-30, NKJV)

*Now it came to pass, as he finished
speaking all these words, that the ground split
apart under them, and the earth opened its
mouth and swallowed them up, with their
households and all the men with Korah, with
all their goods. So they and all those with
them went down alive into the pit; the earth
closed over them, and they perished from
among the assembly.*
(Num. 16:31-33, NKJV)

Moses said that by rejecting his leadership, they were
rejecting the Lord. That is what people do when they dishonor
or make small in their minds, those that God has put in places
of honor in their lives.

*Let everyone be subject to the governing
authorities, for there is no authority except
that which God has established. The
authorities that exist have been established
by God. Consequently, whoever rebels against
the authority is rebelling against what God
has instituted, and those who do so will bring
judgment on themselves.*
(Rom. 13:1-2, NIV)

True authority can never be taken, it can only be given.
Therefore, all real authority is given by God. Too many
believers want all the wonderful things God has to give them,
i.e. their inheritance, BUT they are unwilling to honor those
God has put in their lives. I believe walking in your inheritance
is linked to our ability to honor.

*"Honor your father and your mother, so
that you may live long in the land the LORD
your God is giving you." (Ex. 20:12, NIV)*

God said honor your father and mother that it may be well,
and that you may prolong the days I'm giving you in the land.

The children of Israel were consistently dishonoring to Moses. Every time they grumbled and complained to him, they also mocked and questioned him. Since there was no place in their hearts, for God's leaders, this generation never possessed the place of their inheritance!

Contrast that to the next generation. On the verge of their first invasion into the land under the leadership of Joshua, the leaders of the people came to Joshua encouraging him.

> So, they answered Joshua, saying, "All that
> you command us we will do, and wherever you
> send us we will go. Just as we heeded Moses
> in all things, so we will heed you. Only the
> LORD your God be with you, as He was with
> Moses. Whoever rebels against your command
> and does not heed your words, in all that you
> command him, shall be put to death. Only be
> strong and of good courage."
> (Josh. 1:16-18, NKJV)

Not only did they say we will follow you, they said anyone who doesn't we are taking out. They encouraged Joshua by echoing the very words that the angel of the Lord had spoken to him the previous day, be strong, take courage. They understood that by making space for Joshua as their leader, they would be able to live in the place of their inheritance, and that's just what they did!

Unfortunately, I have known many gifted people who are saved and really do want the promises of God for their lives, and they will do anything to walk in them, except for one thing, they aren't willing to honor certain people. They don't give a space for those who deserve it, whether it's bosses, spouses, church leaders, or the government. They consistently believe they can be dishonoring with no repercussions to their walk with the Lord. Are they saved? Yes. Does God love them? You bet! But because they haven't yet realized the principle of honor they walk just outside the promises, just outside their inheritance.

Again, I encourage you, to allow the Lord to speak to you in this area. You may continually feel like you are in a wilderness crossing, because you haven't yet learned the importance of honoring those around you. Look at each relationship in your life, and ask yourself, am I making the space for them in my heart, that God says they should have?

There is no doubt, the wilderness crossing, is the place of preparation. I've experienced it over and over again in my life. My words, have power, period. My vision and my focus is paramount to going to where God is taking me. And I will only experience honor, to the degree that I am willing to give it to others. The children of Israel couldn't skip these tests and go straight into their inheritance, and neither can we! But by God's grace, we can go through them, and come out on the other side, ready to face the giants and possess the promises!

Chapter 4 – Questions

1. Describe in your own words how and why you think our words have power, and then give an example of how you can use them to effect positive change in either your life or someone else's.

2. Is there a season in your life, that you often look back to as the "best time of your life?" How does it make you feel if your thoughts linger there too long? Is there something about that season that you need to reconcile, that will help you look forward with more excitement and hope?

3. Who do you struggle to honor, or make a place for in your life and why?

SESSION 4 – VIDEO QUESTIONS

1. What season are you looking forward to that God may be preparing you for right now? In what ways is He using your current season to prepare you?

2. Has there ever been a time that you have let shame and regret over previous seasons in your life hold you back from moving forward? What do you think most helps us move past shame and regret?

3. Lynndey, said, "Speak life or speak God over people and situations," what does that look like practically for you?

Chapter 5 – Facing the Giants

One day when I was around twelve years old, I was boarding the bus at the end of the school day. The loading area was busy with lots of other kids trying to get on the bus and find a seat, just like me. I had just reached the top of the bus steps next to the driver's seat, when I heard the familiar taunts of the school bully coming from the back of the bus. I looked past all the kids in the aisle to see who was the object of his torture that day, only to see it was my little brother!

My brother Philip is two years younger than me. He and I have always been close. As an adult, he is one of those people that has a rough exterior, but is a teddy bear on the inside. It's only the years of life that have given him the rough exterior. When he was a kid, he was all teddy bear, sweet, wonderful, playful, and fun.

So there was my little brother, who I love, getting ripped apart by this bully. You could say this kid met all the criteria you can think of when you say the word bully. He was mean, aggressive, and actually very terrifying. You never knew what he would do. He was known to throw punches or get in your face on a whim. Of course he had to ride our bus, so I was very familiar with his ways. And sad to say, this was not the first time my little brother was his target.

Something rose up in me that day when I heard his taunts. I pushed my way through to the back of the bus as quick as I could. When I reached him, I stood square in front of him and smacked him opened handed right across his face! He fell back into the seat, shocked, and so was I! I was never the kind of kid who hit or stood up to anyone!

Immediately after I smacked him, the bus took off, forcing us all down into our seats. I sat down on the aisle across from him with my brother on the side of the window, as if to say, don't come near him or you'll get it again. Another little boy who was in my class and a buddy to me, starting singing, "Lynndey smacked Ryan, Lynndey smacked Ryan." It was music to my ears, and torture to his.

I don't know what got into me that day, for some reason, I wasn't afraid of his retaliation, and for some reason he didn't retaliate. He just sat there quietly. All I can say is I must have had enough! I was sick of his reign of terror and preventing us from having a nice peaceful ride home from school.

I don't condone violence, and don't think kids should hit other kids, but that is what happened that day and it did change things. I can't say the bully completely stopped picking on my brother, but it was with a lot less vitriol and frequency. That was the first of many times in my life, I've had to stand up to something even when it's against my nature, even when I was afraid.

THEY RAN AWAY

One of my favorite Bible teachers, Chuck Missler, used to call Numbers 14 one of the saddest chapters in the Bible. It contains the story of the first generation of the children of Israel refusing to enter their inheritance. Even though I've mentioned their decision a few times, it's important to see how it unfolded. The account goes like this. After about two years of traveling through the wilderness, fighting a couple battles and seeing the supernatural hand of God act on their behalf, God brought them to the edge of their inheritance to camp at a place called Kadesh Barnea. Now, remember these aren't the days of twenty-four seven news, TV, the internet, or newspapers. These people had never seen this land before, so

Moses did what any military commander would do and sent spies into scope out the land.

> *Then Moses sent them to spy out the land*
> *of Canaan, and said to them, "Go up this way*
> *into the South, and go up to the mountains,*
> *and see what the land is like: whether the*
> *people who dwell in it are strong or weak, few*
> *or many; Whether the land they dwell in is*
> *good or bad; whether there are forests there or*
> *not....." (Num. 13:17-20, NKJV)*

The spies were gone for forty days. They returned with an enormous cluster of grapes from a valley they called Eshcol. The congregation saw the grapes, but now it was time to hear the report. What was the land really like?

> *...they brought back word to them and to all*
> *the congregation, and showed them the fruit*
> *of the land. Then they told him, and said: "We*
> *went to the land where you sent us. It truly*
> *flows with milk and honey, and this is its*
> *fruit. Nevertheless, the people who dwell in*
> *the land are strong; the cities are fortified and*
> *very large; moreover, we saw the descendants*
> *of Anak there." (Num. 13:26-28, NKJV)*

I have to imagine the people stood stunned. WHAT? God brought them through all that, and now just when perhaps they thought they could rest, they found out there are giants in the land! Talk about going from a high to a low! As the people were reeling from the report and before another word could be spoken, Caleb one of the twelve spies interjects:

> *Then Caleb quieted the people before*
> *Moses and said, "Let us go up at once **and take***
> ***possession (yarash)** for we are well able to*
> *overcome it." (Num. 13:30, NKJV)*

Even though Caleb was trying to encourage the people, the "bad report" as the scripture calls it, had sunk in. Yes the land was bountiful like God had promised, but it was also filled with giants probably two to three feet taller than them. How were they, a group of ex-slaves an average of five and a half feet tall supposed to drive out several different people groups out of their land?

Though Caleb tried to encourage the people, the other ten spies continued with their bad report.

> *But the men who had gone up with him*
> *said, "We are not able to go up against the*
> *people, for they are stronger than we." and*
> *they gave the children of Israel a bad report of*
> *the land which they had spied out saying, "*
> *The land through which we have gone as spies*
> *is a land that devours its inhabitants and all*
> *the people whom we saw in it are men of great*
> *stature. There we saw the giants (the*
> *descendants of Anak came from the giants);*
> *and we were like grasshoppers in our own*
> *sight, and so we were in their sight."*
> *(Num. 13:31-33, NKJV)*

Up until this point perhaps the people thought the land was just going to fall into their laps. Maybe they imagined their entrance would be under golden arches with roses being thrown at their feet. Now they knew not only was there no welcoming committee, but in fact they were facing a war.

Ten said no, we can't, two said, yes, we can. I haven't done a scientific study on this, but I have to imagine this is probably the same ratio of voices any of us would hear when it comes to facing giants in our lives. Eighty percent of voices inside and out, will tell you, no you can't. What are you thinking? That thing is stronger than you, bigger than you, knows more than you. No, you better not try and take that on. Fear was beginning to grip their hearts. That fear caused them to turn around, missing the promise of their inheritance.

THE GIANT OF FEAR

As a child, I was afraid of the dark. I also had recurring nightmares about people chasing me through the woods and falling off a cliff. I constantly had pictures in my mind of an evil hand reaching up from under my bed and grabbing me. The thing is, I never watched scary movies or opened myself up to the occult in any way, yet my mind was constantly attacked with gripping fear.

When I was twelve I was watching a tv show with my parents and found out what rape was. From then on I was so afraid someone would rape me. As I got older my fear only got worse. Not only was I terrified of something bad happening in the natural I was also afraid of the supernatural. Though my parents never watched horror movies, they sure did like to talk about the supernatural. I would hear stories about famous preachers like Smith Wigglesworth waking up to the Devil in his bedroom. My dad told me that when he was little he saw a demon in his bedroom. All these things certainly didn't help with what I was already dealing with. (Sorry, Mom and Dad, I know you didn't mean it.) I could go on and on about the terrorizing thoughts that consumed me. Funny thing is the only time the fearful thoughts would let up in my life were the times I was not walking with the Lord as a teen and young adult. That should have clued me in on something.

When I became a mother, the fearful thoughts had a new source to torment me with. I would go through seasons where the thoughts were worse and other times where they weren't as bad, but it was a constant battle. I could never be home alone. At night I double checked, even sometimes triple checked, every single window and door before going to bed. Fear was most assuredly a giant in my life that bullied me at will.

FACING FEAR

The season that God was awakening me to my inheritance was a season of increased fear. I was dealing with fearful thoughts off and on all day and night, especially at night. Every time I gave into fear, it would bully me around saying things like, "You can't even go to bed at night without triple locking your doors, you don't trust God." "Who do you think you are, you can't help anyone, you can't even help yourself!" I literally felt it's mocking, just like the taunts of Goliath against Israel.

During this season of increased feelings of fear, I was also feeling the draw of God to press into Him more, to seek the inheritance He was showing me. One morning, I was sitting in my dining room, watching the sun rise over the mountains. In the stillness and quiet of the morning, with my mind's eye, I began to see myself on the banks of the Jordan, just like the children of Israel, peering over into their inheritance. By this time, I was awakening to the same thing they were. I too would have to face a giant to walk in the promises ahead of me. As I continued reading and saw that the children of Israel cowered in fear of their giants, I wondered if I would do the same, as I had so many other times before. Little did I know, the next few moments would change my life as I read God's response to His friend Moses concerning their refusal to enter, their cowering to fear.

> Then the LORD spoke to Moses: "How **long will these people reject Me**? And how long will they not believe Me, with all the signs which I have performed among them?"
> (Num. 14:11, NKJV)

As I read those words, *"How long will these people reject Me,"* it was like I could hear the Father's voice. He was so sad and hurt by their unbelief. He had done all He could to show them, He would protect them, He loved them, He was for them.

82

From His view in heaven, He could see the giants they would have to face, but He could also see the beauty of the inheritance He had for them on the other side. The giants were nothing before God, but His people facing them because they believed Him, were everything to Him in that moment in time.

I had clarity and a realization I had never had before. Every time I obeyed the voice of fear, every time I cowered at its taunts, every time I turned around and ran away, I was rejecting God and forfeiting the beauty that my inheritance contained. My heart sank. I had never until that moment realized that by letting fear bully me around, I was rejecting God. How could I reject God? He saved me from the pit, He rescued me from myself and my sin, how could I reject the One I love? At that moment of clarity I was devastated, yet full of hope at the same time. I dropped to my knees and asked God to forgive me for rejecting Him. I began to declare that He is my God, He is the One who I believe, not fear. As I spent quite a while confessing and repenting, and inviting the blood of Jesus to wash away all the times I came into agreement with fear, I finally slayed my giant. No longer would I bow to its desires, no longer would I obey its voice.

When I share my story about dealing with fear, some reading may think they have never had those kinds of issues with fear. The thing about fear is, it can reach into every sphere of our lives if we let it. While bodily harm to myself, my husband, or my children seemed to have centered around mine, other people's fear giants can take on a different form.

Some people are afraid of being failures or winding up alone. Some people are afraid they will never be loved. Husbands may fear not providing enough for their families. Some people are afraid that their children will turn out poorly, or that they will never get over the loss of a loved one. Some are afraid of sickness and disease. Some people fear rejection, or that they will never "be enough," or that they are "too much." Some people exhaust themselves by people pleasing, or stressing over finances which can also be rooted in fear. Fear can try and plant a seed in every area of life if we allow it to.

The Devil is tricky when it comes to fear. He will convince you that you are just being prudent, being safe sometimes by reacting to fearful thoughts. And the truth is, we need to act wisely in this evil world. But you know how I've come to determine whether a thought or thoughts I'm having are rooted in fear or a warning from God? I ask myself; how do I feel when I think about this? Do I feel empowered? Or, do I feel tormented?

> *There is no fear in love; but perfect love*
> *casts out fear, because fear involves torment.*
> *But he who fears has not been made perfect in*
> *love. (1 John 4:18, NKJV)*

God will never torment you; He will never cause you to worry. If God has a warning for you, or a direction He wants you to take, His Spirit will empower you to act, not torment your mind. I believe God allowed us to see this example of the children of Israel being afraid of the giants, because at the root of almost every giant is some kind of fear. I would say to you, if there are any thoughts that you battle with on a consistent basis, ask yourself, is fear the driving force?

If fear is the root of most giants, then unbelief is the root of fear. Unbelief says God is a liar. Faith says, God is true. Unbelief is not defined by praying for something that never happens, so I must be in unbelief. No, unbelief is when our thoughts and actions don't agree with who God is. Hebrews 3 plainly says, the children of Israel did not enter because of unbelief.

> *And who was it who rebelled against God,*
> *even though they heard his voice? Wasn't it*
> *the people Moses led out of Egypt? And who*
> *made God angry for forty years? Wasn't it the*

people who sinned, whose corpses lay in the
wilderness? And to whom was God speaking
when he took an oath that they would never
enter his rest? Wasn't it the people who
disobeyed him? So, we see that because of
their unbelief they were not able to enter his
rest. (Heb. 3:16-19, NLT)

In the children of Israel's refusal to move forward, they declared with their lives, God is not who He claims to be. That is unbelief. The point of fear is to get us to act like God is not God. This was the foundation of Satan's rebellion, the accusation that **God should not be God.**

You could say Satan and the angels who followed him rejected God's Godship. Satan thought he should be God instead. Satan did exactly what God said the children of Israel were doing by obeying fear, rejecting God. That is what fear entices us to do. That is why Satan loves to try and make you afraid, he wants you to agree with him and he uses intimidation as his weapon.

OUR FAITH

When we looked to God for our salvation, in a way we sat at a covenant table with Him, much like the children of Israel sat at the foot of Mt Sinai. God came to the covenant table with EVERYTHING, including eternal life and our inheritance in His Kingdom. Most people like to say we came to the table with nothing, but that's not true. Each person who comes to the table of salvation comes with something, our faith. A faith that says God is who He claims to be, the only One who can save through His Son Jesus.

But without faith it is impossible to please
him: for he that cometh to God must believe

that he is, and that he is a rewarder of them
that diligently seek him. (Heb. 11:6, KJV)

That morning as I tearfully repented to the Father for rejecting Him and agreeing that fear was greater than Him, I also began to yarash my inheritance. I have continued to walk free from fear's hold, which is part of my inheritance. Freedom is our inheritance!

Since that day, I have still been attacked by the spirit of fear, many times. I have even given into its voice, by acting on fear instead of faith a few times. Even when I mess up, I remember that we have three things at our constant disposal that are far greater than any giant. Our three giant defeating weapons are confession, repentance, and the blood of Jesus. Since that day, if I sin against God by acting in fear, I confess it and repent- meaning turn back around to walking forward in faith. I no longer let fear dictate my life! That giant has been defeated by the blood of the Lamb. Whatever giant you may be facing, whatever may be standing between you and the beckoning of the Lord to move forward, ask yourself have I agreed with something that says God is not who He says He is? If so, confess it and repent. Jesus's blood plus nothing wins. Live a lifestyle of confessing God's word over your life and your situations. Declare that what God says is true. It's time to face the giants and yarash your inheritance!

Though Joshua and Caleb continued to try and encourage the children of Israel, they refused to move forward in the face of the giants in the land. Fear had its way by gripping their hearts and paralyzing their feet.

So, all the congregation lifted up their
voices, and cried, and the people wept that
night. And all the children of Israel
complained against Moses and Aaron, and the
whole congregation said to them, "If only we
had died in the land of Egypt! Or if only we

had died in this wilderness! "Why has the
LORD brought us to this land to fall by the
sword, that our wives and children should
become victims? Would it not be better for us
to return to Egypt?" So, they said to one
another, "Let us select a leader and return to
Egypt." (Num. 14:1-4, NKJV)

That generation never got to experience the beauty of their inheritance during their lives. Both God and the children of Israel lost something that day. The children of Israel lost the privilege they had to live in a land flowing with milk and honey, and God lost the glory He gets when His children live lives that declare that He is God.

CHAPTER 5 – QUESTIONS

1. Have you ever struggled with fear, and if so what is the specific object of your fear? Do you think that fear is just something you will always deal with, or do you think it's something that God wants to rid from your life?

2. What form have giants taken in your life?

3. What part of God's character do you believe you need to know more in order to help combat any fear you experience?

SESSION 5 – VIDEO QUESTIONS

1. Why do you think even after salvation, there are certain things we have to overcome in life? In other words, why doesn't God just snap His fingers and everything in our lives becomes easy?

2. Can you identify any strongholds in your mind that began developing as a child?

3. What are some truths you know about God that you can arm yourself with as you run toward your giant?

Chapter 6 – Eye on the Prize

*Not that I have already obtained all this, or
already have arrived at my goal, but I press
on to lay hold of that for which Christ has laid
hold of me. Brothers and sisters I do not
consider myself yet to have taken hold of it.
But one thing I do; Forgetting what is behind
and straining towards what is ahead, I press
on towards the goal, to win the prize for which
God has called me Heavenward in Christ
Jesus. All of us, then, who are mature should
take such a view of things.
(Phil.3:12-15, NIV)*

Were you the kind of kid who wouldn't stop asking your mom or dad for something until they said yes? Have you ever fixed your eye on a goal in life so intently that you didn't stop until you reached it? Have you ever had to persevere in the face of difficult circumstances when the only thing that kept you going was pure determination you were going to get to the other side? That's how God wants us to be about our inheritance!

For many of us however, life's disappointments and let downs have caused us to lose some of the tenacity we once had to press on towards the things of God like Paul did. Paul calls this don't stop, can't stop attitude, a mature mind. Becoming mature in the Lord, is part of our inheritance. But, because pursuing maturity will be messy at times, many shrink back, in the age of everything I do must look good enough to put on social media. We must be willing to take the risk of not looking perfect all the time, learn from our falls, get back up, and press ahead to become mature. Maturity should be a goal of every believer, not the elite few.

After I had been ministering for a couple years locally, my pastor, Mike Murray advised me to consider joining an apostolic fellowship. Joining a fellowship has many benefits, like a prayer covering, the members support, and becoming licensed to minister. I took his advice and applied to the same fellowship he belonged to, Maranatha Ministerial Fellowship, International. Never having been a part of something like that before I didn't know how comprehensive the process to join would be. I needed to obtain several personal references from spiritual leaders, write about my calling, and at the end I sat with the entire apostolic board, and told them everything about my life, the good the bad and the ugly. The board was full of love and wisdom, and cheerfully accepted me into the fellowship. Chris and I were delighted!

A few months later, at the annual conference I was officially licensed and received the laying on of hands and prophetic words. Bishop Rick Callahan, the founder of the fellowship prayed and spoke over me first then the rest who felt lead went in turn. After everyone was done, seemingly compelled by the Spirit, Bishop said one more thing to me. He said "And Lynndey, God is going to set aside time in your life and ministry to write." In that moment I thought, I don't even like writing! And time, where would I get that? I was so busy homeschooling my kids and doing ministry with Free Hearts, when would I have time to write?

Fast forward nine months later, at God's invitation our family moved to Tennessee, a state neither Chris nor I had ever set foot in! With Chris and the kids gone all day, and absolutely nothing to do, I opened up my notebook and began to write this book! I thought to myself, God You are funny! I guess You know how to make time in my life and ministry for me to write! As I sit here three years later, probably having written the book ten times, it's finally in editing! I'm almost done.

91

I know this book and what will become of it are part of my inheritance. But in order to pursue it I had to press on even when I didn't know what I was doing. I have wanted to quit writing at least a dozen times, but every time the Holy Spirit would impress upon me the importance of keeping on keeping on. Every time, I walked away from my computer saying to myself "I can't do this," a little later I would pick it back up with the nudging of the Holy Spirit saying," I know you can't, but I can in you."

I want to be a person who is so determined to do what Jesus has asked me to do no matter how hard, or even how imperfect it may be that my kids say, "Wow, look at my mom, I'm going to press towards Jesus like her!" Jesus is asking us to be determined to possess yourself, what God has already determined you can have, your inheritance! In this chapter, I want to show you some examples of those who did and did not cherish their inheritance by going after it. I believe not only will you learn a lot from them, but also see how much it means to God, that we keep on keeping on, that we pursue, that we yarash, all that He has for us in this life!

TWO BROTHERS

Esau and Jacob were the twin sons of the patriarch Isaac. Some twins get along like best friends, while others fight. These two fought and it began before they were born!

> *Now Isaac pleaded with the LORD for his wife, because she was barren; and the LORD granted his plea, and Rebekah his wife conceived. But the children struggled together within her... (Gen. 25: 21-22, NKJV)*

At the center of Jacob's and Esau's lifelong fight was the first born's nachal, inheritance. In the ancient Hebrew culture the firstborn's inheritance was double the size of every other son's! Meaning if there were four sons, at the father's death, the inheritance would be divided equally into five portions. The firstborn would receive the extra portion, giving him a double portion of the inheritance.

Another privilege the firstborn had was to assume the patriarchal position of the family after the father's death. The Hebrews believed the strongest of the father's strength was placed inside his first born son at conception, making him the most fit to lead the family at the father's death. Leading the family and the double portion were the nachal right of the firstborn. Even at their birth, Jacob and Esau struggled over who would come out first, or who would receive the firstborn's nachal inheritance.

> *So, when her days were fulfilled for her to give birth, indeed there were twins in her womb. And the first came out red. He was like a hairy garment all over; so, they called his name Esau. Afterward, his brother came out, and his hand took hold of Esau's heel; so, his name was called Jacob.*
> *(Gen. 25: 24-26, NKJV)*

There is no doubt that the struggle their mother felt in her womb was that of the brothers positioning themselves as to who would enter the birth canal first! Jacob didn't get there in time, but that didn't stop him from continuing to try. Can you imagine his tiny little hand grabbing hold of his brother's heel? That's how deeply the desire to possess the first born inheritance was in Jacob's heart even at birth. And it didn't stop there. Jacob's desire for the firstborn's inheritance continued on with him into manhood.

> *Now Jacob cooked a stew; and Esau came in from the field, and he was weary. And Esau said to Jacob, "Please feed me with that same red stew, for I am weary." Therefore, his name*

*was called Edom. But Jacob said, "Sell me
your birthright as of this day." And Esau said,
"Look, I am about to die; so what is this
birthright to me?" Then Jacob said, Swear to
me as of this day." So he swore to him, and
sold his birthright to Jacob. And Jacob gave
Esau bread and stew of lentils; then he ate
and drank, arose, and went his way. **Thus
Esau despised his birthright.**
(Gen. 25: 29-34, NKJV)*

In that moment of weakness Esau sold his special nachal
inheritance, not for riches, not for love, but for stew! Instead of
Esau, Jacob would now have the double portion inheritance.
Jacob would be the patriarch of the family, and most of all,
Jacob would inherit the promises of God made to his
grandfather Abraham. Now Jacob had what he wanted since
before he was born.

Jacob was so zealous in fact for the birthright that he was
willing to lie, manipulate, and to trick anyone, including his
father just so he could have the firstborn inheritance. You
would think for all Jacob's dishonesty God would have been
angry with him. But interestingly, that is not what the
scripture says God thinks of Jacob, in fact, He says the
opposite!

*As it is written "Jacob I have loved, but
Esau I have hated." (Rom. 9:13, NKJV)*

God loves Jacob, but hates Esau? This verse seems to go
against everything that God stands for. Why would God love
the one who tricked and lied to get what he wanted? This is
where we need a full view of who God is and what He's about.

I've heard this verse explained to say that Paul is talking
about the election of God. In other words, God can choose who
He wants and who He does not. Another explanation is that
God isn't really saying He hates Esau, He is just highlighting

that He has chosen Jacob to carry on the covenant promises instead. There is truth in both those statements, **but I also believe God's comment reflects what He thinks about the difference in how the brothers valued the inheritance.** One brother was willing to yarash for it, or take it by force while the other threw it away for stew!

God loves all His children all the time, we can't earn His love, we don't do anything to deserve His love. But like any father, God is not always pleased with His children's decisions or actions. God was not pleased with the first generation of Hebrews who would not enter into their inheritance. *(Heb.3 & 1 Cor.10)* Neither was He pleased with Esau who despised his firstborn inheritance.

In the moment that Esau, sold Jacob his birthright, the scripture says, Esau despised his birthright. The Hebrew word for despised, bazah, means to regard as worthless, to make something of little or no value, to treat something or someone like nothing. By giving away his birthright Esau was saying he didn't care enough about his God given inheritance to go hungry a little bit longer. Esau's attitude was in direct contrast to Jacob's who'd been fighting since before he was born to possess the birthright!

In contrast to Esau, Jacob didn't let the circumstances around his birth stop him from fighting for the prized possession of the inheritance until he possessed it! That is the same spirit I believe Paul was talking about when he compared himself as a runner who runs to win and as a person pressing towards the prize.

God wants us to desire what He has for us, our inheritance. To understand why it's so important to Him, is to understand the link between God and His creation. God is the author of all life and all that is good. So to simply dismiss what He has apportioned to us in our inheritance like Esau did, is like dismissing Him.

God said I love Jacob because Jacob loved the things that God had promised for Abraham's family, even when by birth they rightly belonged to his brother! He said he hated Esau, because by despising his birthright, He was despising God. Remember, God is the One who ordered their birth. It wasn't happenstance that Esau was born first. At his birth, God designed for Esau to have the firstborn's birthright. But Esau did not value what God set apart for him. By treating his birthright as nothing, Esau was treating God the same way!

That is a sobering thought when it comes to how we see our inheritance in Him. I believe that our inheritance isn't something we should treat lightly, or think, yeah that sounds good, but I'm happy right here in the wilderness of wandering. No! I believe God wants us to do the opposite of bazah when it comes to our inheritance, we need to esteem the things that God has set apart for us in this life, which is thereby esteeming Him. We are to imitate the Apostle Paul like he told us by keeping our eyes on the prize of God and the upward call of Christ Jesus in this life!

CALEB THE SON OF JEPHUNNEH

Caleb, the son of Jephunneh, was one of the twelve spies sent into the land of Canaan when the first generation arrived on the borders of their inheritance. When the spies returned to camp and gave the discouraging report, saying there was no way they could defeat the giants or conquer the large cities in the land, Caleb was only one of two that said, yes we can!

> *And Caleb stilled the people before Moses,*
> *and said, Let us go up at once, **and possess***
> ***it;(yarash)** for we are **well able to overcome***
> ***it.(yarash)** (Num. 13:30, NKJV)*

Notice Caleb's words, let us go up at once! The walk between Egypt and the wilderness crossing had done its work in Caleb's heart. Caleb was ready to go in the land. Caleb said, we can dispossess them, and take our rightful inheritance. It didn't seem to cross Caleb's mind for a moment that they couldn't do it, he said, "We are **well able** to overcome it!"

The name Caleb means, faithful, wholehearted, bold, and brave. That is exactly who this Caleb was. Caleb's wholeheartedly devoted and brave spirit is the "different spirit" God made mention of when He said, Caleb would be one of only two that could come back to the land.

> *But my servant Caleb, because he has a*
> *different spirit in him and has followed Me*
> *fully, I will bring him into the land where he*
> *went and his descendants shall inherit it.*
> *(Num. 14:24, NKJV)*

Sadly for Caleb, though he was ready to enter the land, he had to turn around and walk through that wilderness of wandering for almost forty years until all that generation died, except him and Joshua. After those forty years, you might think Caleb had lost a little bit of his spunk, when it came time to yarashing his inheritance. But, he didn't. When He came back around forty years later he reminded Joshua, I've already picked out my mountain, you just need to let me loose on these giants so I can go get it!

> *Then the children of Judah came to Joshua*
> *in Gilgal. And Caleb the son of Jephunneh the*
> *Kenizzite said to him: "You know the word*
> *which the LORD said to Moses the man of God*
> *concerning you and me in Kadesh Barnea. I*
> *was forty years old when Moses the servant of*
> *the LORD sent me from Kadesh Barnea to spy*
> *out the land, and I brought back word to him*
> *as it was in my heart. Nevertheless my*
> *brethren who went up with me made the*
> *heart of the people melt, but I wholly followed*

the LORD my God. So Moses swore on that
day, saying, 'Surely the land where your foot
has trodden shall be your inheritance and
your children's forever, because you have
wholly followed the LORD my God.' And now,
behold, the LORD has kept me alive, as He
said, these forty-five years, ever since the
LORD spoke this word to Moses while Israel
wandered in the wilderness; and now, here I
am this day, eighty-five years old. **As yet I am**
as strong this day as on the day that Moses
sent me; just as my strength was then, so now
is my strength for war, both for going out and
for coming in. *Now therefore, give me this*
mountain of which the LORD spoke in that
day; for you heard in that day how the
Anakim were there, and that the cities were
great and fortified. It may be that the LORD
will be with me, and I shall be able to drive
them out as the LORD said." And Joshua
blessed him, and gave Hebron to Caleb the
son of Jephunneh as an inheritance.
(Josh. 14:6-13, NKJV)

Caleb didn't let the wilderness wandering take him out. At
the second chance he said, I am just as strong now at eighty as
I was at forty! Neither age, discouragement, or time, was going
to stop Caleb from going after his promised inheritance from
God! That is a great encouragement for any of us who feel like
we've spent more time in the wilderness of wandering than we
wanted to. So did Caleb, but he kept his devotion to the Lord
and when the time came around again he didn't shrink back.
He trusted, if God is with me, I can drive out those giants. No
matter our age, no matter our past, no matter how long we
have wandered, if we believe that God is with us, we too can
come out of the wilderness wandering and begin to possess the
promises of God for our lives.

Caleb is also a great example to those who feel they have been in the wilderness wandering because of their connection to someone else. I know many spouses who are either married to non-believers or believers who aren't motivated at all to grow in God. Caleb could have shrunk back after all the time he spent in the wilderness, because of the first generation. But Caleb didn't let who he was linked to discourage him. We also don't ever see him curse the first generation, of whom I'm sure his parents and all his friends belonged. No, He waited patiently until God brought him back around to the promise. I have to believe that it was Caleb's unwavering faith in God that sustained him all those years. We call Hebrews 11 the great hall of faith, and Caleb is indirectly mentioned there because it says, *"By faith the walls of Jericho fell down, after they were compassed about seven days.(Heb. 11: 30, NKJV)* Caleb was there, marching around the walls of Jericho, in faith. Faith is the substance of things hoped for, the evidence of things not seen. So if you have been in Caleb's shoes, keep believing, keep hoping, keep building your faith, because God's going to bring you back around to the promises. It's not too late.

ACHSAH DAUGHTER OF CALEB

As a little girl, I imagine Achsah, Caleb's daughter following her dad around as much as she was able. She might have even been considered a daddy's girl. No matter the circumstances of her childhood, one thing is for sure, she ended up with her father's spirit. And though she grew up in the wilderness of wandering, when the time came for them to enter the land, like her father, Achsah had her eye on the prize.

Once the Israelites invaded the land, Caleb didn't waste any time getting into the mountains of Hebron and kicking giant butt. He defeated three giant brothers, Sheshai, Ahiman, and Talmai, then he set his eyes on another city, Kirjath Sepher. He promised Achsah's hand in marriage to the man who would attack the city and kill its inhabitants. Caleb's nephew stepped up, took the city and won his bride. The nephew didn't just gain a wife, he gained a woman with a tenacious spirit, one like her dad's.

> *Now it was so, when she came to him, that she persuaded him to ask her father for a field. So she dismounted from her donkey, and Caleb said to her, "What do you wish?" She answered, "Give me a blessing; since you have given me land in the South, give me also springs of water." So he gave her the upper springs and the lower springs.*
> *(Josh. 15:18-19, NKJV)*

Achsah, already had the blessing of the south, the Negev, but she wanted more! You might be tempted to think she was greedy; however, the scripture never seems to imply that it was wrong for her to ask for more. In fact, I believe her father rewarded her boldness by giving her the upper and the lower springs. Notice that it says, he gave them to **her**. Not that they weren't meant for her and the family, but the honor goes to her. The scripture never gets a word wrong. I believe it says "her" on purpose because God wanted to highlight this woman's heart in wanting a greater inheritance. In fact this account was recorded not once, but twice in scripture (Joshua and Judges).

Caleb's heart to reward his daughter mirrors the heart of the Father towards us when we are bold to ask Him for more of an inheritance. God wants us to want the inheritance because when we do, we are saying, I value what you have for me God. I value the plan that you have for my life. We are saying, Your plans and Your ways are better. Can we ever really ever have enough when it comes to what God has for us?

THE DAUGHTERS OF ZELOPHEHAD

During the wilderness crossing, God instructed Moses to take a census of the people. The purpose of the census was to find out how many families were represented in each tribe. By knowing how big each individual tribe was, then Moses could divvy out a specific portion of land to each tribe according to how many families they contained.

> *"To these the land shall be divided as an inheritance, according to the number of names. To the large tribe you shall give a larger inheritance, and to a small tribe you shall give a smaller inheritance. Each shall be given its inheritance according to those who were numbered of them, But the land shall be divided by lot; they shall inherit according to the names of the tribes of their fathers."*
> *(Num. 26:52-55, NKJV)*

Throughout the scriptures, families are named and counted by the men. Likewise inheritances were only passed through men, meaning women did not normally inherit. When the reason for the census was made known, five daughters of a man named Zeolphehad quickly realized this would have a great impact on them as their father had no sons. So they went to Moses with a request;

> *Then came the daughters of Zelophehad the son of Hepher, the son of Gilead, the son of Machir, the son of Manasseh, ...And they stood before Moses, before Eleazar the priest, and before the leaders and all the congregation, by the doorway of the tabernacle of meeting, saying: "Our father died in the wilderness; but he was not in the company of those who gathered together against the LORD, in company with Korah, but he died in*

his own sin; and he had no sons. Why should
the name of our father be removed from
among his family because he had no son? Give
us a possession among our father's brothers."
So Moses brought their case before the LORD.
(Num. 27:1-5, NKJV)

These ladies had no precedent for what they were asking.
All they knew was that if they weren't willing **to dispossess the
normal precedent** by asking for a new one, they definitely
weren't going to have an inheritance when they arrived at the
Promised Land.

And the LORD spoke to Moses, saying: "The
daughters of Zelophehad speak what is right;
you shall surely give them a possession of
inheritance among their father's brothers, and
cause the inheritance of their father to pass to
them.
(Num. 27:6-7, NKJV)

Their father's share of inherited land was granted to them.
Again the Lord rewarded their desire and their boldness to go
after their inheritance. However, because of the first
generation's refusal to enter the land, forty years went by after
this scene. Upon the arrival at the edge of the land of Canaan
again, the sisters realized that they would once again have to
contend with the new leaders for what God already said they
could have.

But Zelophehad the son of Hepher, the son
of Gilead, the son of Machir, the son of
Manasseh, had no sons, but only daughters.
And these are the names of his daughters:
Mahlah, Noah, Hoglah, Milcah, and Tirzah.
And they came near before Eleazar the priest,
before Joshua the son of Nun, and before the
rulers, saying, "The LORD commanded Moses
to give us an inheritance among our brothers."

102

Therefore, according to the commandment of
the LORD, he gave them an inheritance among
their father's brothers.
(Josh.17:3-4, NKJV)

Not once but twice these ladies fought for their inheritance. I've heard it said that God is obligated to fulfill His promises but not our potential. God is looking to give to those who value what He has to give.

I've been showing you examples of who we should be like, Jacob, Caleb, Achsah and the daughters of Zeoplphad, while the writer of Hebrews takes a different approach. The writer of Hebrews shows us who **NOT TO BE LIKE,** the generation who didn't possess their inheritance.

Who were they who heard and rebelled?
Were they not all those Moses had led out of
Egypt? And with whom was he angry for forty
years? Was it not with those who sinned,
whose bodies perished in the wilderness? And
to whom did God swear that they would never
enter his rest if not to those who disobeyed?
So we see that they were not able to enter,
because of their unbelief.

Therefore, since the promise of entering his
rest still stands, let us be careful that none of
you be found to have fallen short of it. For we
also have had the good news proclaimed to us,
just as they did; but the message they heard
was of no value to them, because they did not
share the faith of those who obeyed. Now we
who have believed enter that rest, just as God
has said,

"So I declared on oath in my anger, 'They
shall never enter my rest.'

*And yet his works have been finished since
the creation of the world. For somewhere he
has spoken about the seventh day in these
words: "On the seventh day God rested from
all his works."
(Heb. 3:16-19 & 4:1-4, NIV)*

THE DAY MY WORLD CHANGED FOREVER

Held within this warning is something very powerful and profound, that I have only recently grabbed hold of. The day I saw it, I wrote at the top of my journal, "The day my world changed forever!" This revelation is a key to walking in your inheritance like none other! I saw this key after meditating on the last three verses at the end of the book of Hebrews, warning to not be like the generation who refused to enter their inheritance.

*"...So I swore in my wrath, They shall not
enter My rest although the works were
finished from the foundation of the world "For
somewhere he has spoken about the seventh
day in these words: "On the seventh day God
rested from all his works."
(Heb. 4:3-4 NKJV)*

To really understand this verse, we have to understand what God means when He's talking about "His rest." He refers to "His rest", a total of ten times between Hebrews 3 & 4. Though God keeps saying they didn't enter His rest, the account He is obviously referring to is about the children of Israel not entering their inheritance, the land of Canaan.

So what is the "rest" God is talking about that He is paralleling to entering their inheritance? The answer to what this "rest" is, can be found in verse 4, *"For He has spoken in a certain place of the seventh day in this way: And God rested on the seventh day from all His works"* God is comparing them entering their inheritance to the seventh day of creation, when God rested.

I believe what God is saying is that they could have entered their inheritance with the same attitude He displayed on the seventh day of creation, rest. God stood on the seventh day looking back, seeing that He had already made a way during the six days of creation for them to enter their promised inheritance, *"the works were finished from the foundation of the world."*

The children of Israel could have entered their inheritance with a heart full of rest, knowing the way was already made by God. Finished means having been completed, or ended. Their ability to enter was already completed, all they had to do was believe. Friend, God is making the same invitation to us. He says,

> *"Today if you will hear His voice, Do not harden your hearts..."There remains therefore a rest of the people of God."*
> *(Heb. 4:7 & 9, NKJV)*

As we move towards our inheritance, we can enter the same type of rest that God entered on the seventh day of creation knowing that the way has already been made for us. In fact, God wrote all the days of our lives in a book before we were born, preparing the steps we should take.

> *Your eyes saw my unformed body; all the days ordained for me were written in your book before one of them came to be.*
> *(Psalm 139:16, NIV)*

> *For we are His workmanship, created in Christ Jesus for good works, which God prepared beforehand that we should walk in them. (Eph 2:10, NKJV)*

God is inviting us to live in a place of rest. It's from that position of REST that we can actually walk through our lives. We can enter the same rest as God did on the seventh day of creation, even while we yarash, knowing that it's already done!

When God showed me the invitation to live in the rest knowing it's all already been done, I literally danced around my house for the next three days! I think my husband thought I was being a little weird. But to every challenge that came up, to every worrisome thought that tried to lodge in my mind, to everything for weeks, I said, "It's already done, it's already done." Can you imagine the lightness you could walk in everyday of your life, knowing that in every circumstance, every action, even in times of pressing, it's already done? Please mark this spot in your book and come back to it next time you feel overwhelmed so you can remember, we are invited to live in the rest of God.

Even in the hours before Jesus's arrest, He lived from a place of rest. He knew that if He laid down His life, He would rise again. He knew if He separated from the Father by taking our sins, He would be reunited with Him. He looked past the cross knowing His victory was already won.

CHAPTER 6 – QUESTIONS

1. Why do you think it's so important to God for you to pursue your inheritance, or the things He has called you to in this life?

2. Many suffer from anxiety, which is usually an overwhelming sense of pressure and things feeling out of control. In light of knowing that God's portion for us is rest, what kind of weight does that take off you to perform or get things accomplished?

3. How do you reconcile the paradox of "taking action" from a place of rest? How do you see that playing out in your life?

SESSION 6 – VIDEO QUESTIONS

1. What's the best way to determine the quality of the things you are hearing?

2. What do you think Lynndey meant when she said, "We are to see something first by faith, before you see it in the natural?"

3. What situation in your life right now, do you need understanding for the most?

Chapter 7 – It's Not All About You!

When the second generation of Israelites were led by God, back to the borders of the land of Canaan they must have been ecstatic to be so close to finally having a home! After almost forty years of wandering in the wilderness, they were beginning to get a glimpse of their long awaited inheritance, the land flowing with milk and honey. While they put down camp near the banks of the Jordan, in Gilgal, the leaders of Reuben, Gad, and half the tribe of Manassah looked around and thought the land on the Eastern side of the Jordan looked pretty good to them. In fact it wasn't just ok, they agreed, it would actually be perfect for their families and livestock! As anyone would, they began to wonder why they should go through all the hassle of crossing the Jordan if the place where they already were was so perfect? Confident in the sensibility of their request, they approached Moses with this proposal:

> *The Reubenites and Gadites, who had very large herds and flocks, saw that the lands of Jazer and Gilead were suitable for livestock. 2 So they came to Moses and Eleazar the priest and to the leaders of the community, and said... the land the Lord subdued before the people of Israel—are suitable for livestock, and your servants have livestock. 5 If we have found favor in your eyes," they said, "let this land be given to your servants as our possession. Do not make us cross the Jordan."*
> *(Num. 32:1-5, NIV)*

As I've shown you, desiring your inheritance from God is a good thing. When other's like the daughters of Zelophehad, and Achsah requested an inheritance, it was like God applauded them by rewarding their request. I believe God would have done the same here except their proposal had a little twist to it that God and Moses didn't see so favorably. *"Do not make us cross the Jordan,"* they said. The leaders of these tribes, wanted to stay back and start settling into their lives, as the rest of the tribes marched forward to a certain battle with giants.

> *Moses said to the Gadites and Reubenites,*
> *"Should your fellow Israelites go to war while*
> *you sit here? Why do you discourage the*
> *Israelites from crossing over into the land the*
> *Lord has given them? This is what your*
> *fathers did when I sent them from Kadesh*
> *Barnea to look over the land. After they went*
> *up to the Valley of Eshkol and viewed the*
> *land, they discouraged the Israelites from*
> *entering the land the Lord had given*
> *them....... "And here you are, a brood of*
> *sinners, standing in the place of your fathers*
> *and making the Lord even more angry with*
> *Israel...... (Num. 32:6-14, NIV)*

I can imagine Moses picturing that generation doing the same thing their parents had as he shouted, that not going with their brothers could possibly cause the tribes to falter again. What a travesty that would have been!

Whether we mean for them to or not, our actions or inactions affect others' lives in very powerful ways. What we do and say in our everyday lives and conversations, has the ability to throw courage onto someone, or pull courage off them. From the two and half tribe's request, Moses saw a people whose only concern was for their own inheritance, having little thought to how their actions would affect their fellow Israelites.

WHAT A FRIEND CAN DO

Have you ever had a friend who would jump off a cliff with you? Have you ever had a friend so loyal and faithful to you that they were always wanting the best for you, no matter what? My sister-in law Susan was that friend for me. Although we had been sisters-in-law for years, our friendship really formed when our family moved to Vermont in 2008. I remember the first few years I lived there, I would go to her house for coffee and sit and just share with her whatever the Lord was showing me in the scriptures. She would usually say with great enthusiasm, "You have to teach that to other people!" We often told people that the ministry we began years later was born out of our friendship, and in many ways it was.

Fast forward a few years later, Susan and I were having our weekly Free Hearts planning session one morning. It was late summer so we were on her front porch with our coffee trying to catch some sunshine before winter set in. Free Hearts had been going for about a year at that point and we were both in a posture of just asking God to show us what was next.

On that particular morning, Susan said to me, "I've been praying and I feel like you need to ask your pastor if we can hold a one day women's event at your church." I remember the distinct feeling that I was not qualified enough to make this request. Up until then, we had mainly been ministering in homes to a very small number of women. It would require a lot of courage for me to make an appointment with my pastors and ask to lead a women's meeting intended for several churches. But with her encouragement, I did, and so we went!

As we sat down with my pastors the following week, I nervously shared with them our desire to host a whole day women's event with teachings, worship, prayer, and a catered lunch. To our delight, Pastor Mike and Pastor Mary, gave us an enthusiastic yes! After we talked through a few details, Pastor

111

Mary stopped and looked at me with a sweet smile. I could tell she had something to share. She told us that she had actually already wanted to invite Free Hearts to host an event at the church but, when she prayed about asking us, the Lord told her to "Wait until she asks."

In that moment, I began to understand this great power that we all possess, the power of encouragement. What if, Susan had never thrown the courage on me that day to ask? I'm not sure it would have ever happened. Something happens when a friend comes alongside you in life and supports your gifts. Suddenly, you can do things, you would have never been able to accomplish on your own. I've been blessed to have many friends like that in my life who have thrown courage on me, just when I needed it!

That particular event that Susan encouraged me to ask for, was more than we ever hoped it would be. It was a turning point in the life of Free Hearts Ministries. God used that day to establish us in a way that He needed, to get us to the next place in His plan. Which was the ability to minister to many more people in ways neither of us could ever have imagined.

Encourage literally means to throw courage on someone. What Susan gave me that day, and many other days was the courage to face the unknown and go for it with God. She helped me be bold when I wanted to be timid. She didn't just encourage me to do things, she went with me. Because we crossed over the unknown together we were able to keep going even when we didn't know what we were doing! All that Susan and I were blessed to be able to do with Free Hearts while I was in Vermont, was part of our inheritance. One of Susan's favorite Bible verses to quote during that time was; *Two are better than one, because they have a good return for their labor. (Ecc. 4:9, NIV)*

We need each other's, YOU CAN DO IT, to yarash our inheritance, and Moses knew that. It was the discouraging

112

words from ten spies that their fathers listened to forty years earlier that stopped them from entering the land. You and I have the power to help others go forward in the things of God, or pull them back! So, may we be people that constantly remind each other of this truth: *"I can do all things through Christ who strengthens me." (Phil 4:13, NKJV)*

PRACTICALLY SPEAKING – WHAT DOES THIS LOOK LIKE?

I never like to throw something out there that the Lord asks of us without offering a practical way to respond. You've probably already asked yourself these two questions, first, who is the "who" we are supposed to help, because we can't help everyone? And secondly, how do we help people? The answers to who and how are simpler than you may think.

First let me point out that Moses wasn't looking around for someone outside of the Israelite family to help the other tribes, he was looking at those who were already on the same journey with them. The "who" you're called to help are those currently in your life, those walking next to you. In my own example, Susan and I were doing life together, we were family but also friends.

We all need to recognize that the people in our lives aren't there by accident, but by design. Then we can begin to awaken to the fact that we actually have the ability to influence them for good. To the degree that people will allow you, and to the degree that God shows you, just be willing to help those around you move towards God and towards their inheritance, whatever that looks like.

When I think about the power that our encouragement can have on each other, to face the unknown for the sake of the Kingdom, my mind goes to a few game changing accounts in the scripture. Had it not been for Mordecai's persistent encouragement to Queen Ester, to go in and see the King, to reveal Haman's evil plot against the Jews, would she have done it? And then there is Jonathan's support of David. Right as Saul was beginning to formulate a plan to kill David, it was Jonathan, who threw the courage onto David, to rebel against the King and run away. That decision, saved young David's life. Even, Jesus, had a heavenly encouragement session with Elijah and Moses, who spoke to Jesus about His death on the Mount of Transfiguration.

In John 17:12 it's recorded, that Jesus prayed, "*Those who You gave Me, I have kept; and none of them is lost, except the son of perdition.*" Jesus, saw the disciples as those who God gave to Him, during His earthly life. As such, He threw courage on each of them in just the way they needed, to walk in the fullness of the life God intended for them. It was part of Peter's inheritance to preach on the Day of Pentecost when 3,000 people were saved. But had Jesus not gone to the beach to restore Peter after he denied Him, would Peter have made it to that point? There were many times, Jesus, crossed over and fought for His brethren during His life. Even when they all deserted Him, Jesus was still fighting for them.

There isn't a magic formula as to how much or how little you help certain people, just ask the Holy Spirit, "Who have you given me and how can I help them?" Begin to look around, and see who is going in the same direction as you, and help pull them along. Seek to understand more fully, how powerful this thing is that we all have at the tip of our tongues, the power of encouragement, and start using it!

HOW?

Since the "how" could be a countless number of specific ways, I'll keep it very easy. Don't be selfish! Don't be self-centered. Don't think everything in your life or someone else's is all about you. I say this so boldly and emphatically because

114

most of us tend to be this way, including me. Helping someone else goes against our "me" nature, it goes against our "look out for number one" mentality, it goes against everything in this world, except for God's way. Even Jesus while He was clearly on a mission to claim His inheritance said:

> *"For even the Son of Man did not come to be served, but to serve, and to give His life a ransom for many." (Mark 10:45, NKJV)*

Something remarkable happens when you help others that you might not expect, you are simultaneously helping yourself! In the natural, we're tempted to think if we're helping someone else, then we're giving up time and effort to spend on our own pursuits. But the Kingdom of God doesn't work like that! Moses told the two and a half tribes, if you go help them, then yours will be there to come back to. It's the same principle that Jesus gave when He said. *"For whoever desires to save his life will lose it, but whoever loses his life for My sake will find it." (Matt. 16:25, NKJV)* God's Kingdom is the opposite of the world's, whenever we give, we don't lose, but receive back much more!

Jesus has called us to lose our self-seeking nature, to deny our own ambitions, and to invest in His Kingdom, which is made up of people. When Jesus denied His flesh to die on the cross, it was His self-sacrificing act that caused Him to become the King of Kings, part of His inheritance! Sacrifice for others is the path to our inheritance.

IT'S ACTUALLY SIN

Moses told the tribes that requested to stay back, *"But if you fail to do this, you will be sinning against the LORD; and you may be sure that your sin will find you out." (Num.32:23, NIV)*

This was Moses's stern warning to the two and a half tribes that didn't "have" to cross over and fight the Canaanites. This brings me to my last point on this matter, God calls it sin when we refuse to help others. You may think this sounds harsh, but if we actually think about what God is expecting the Israelites to do, we will see why God calls it a sin.

In my mind inheritance = Kingdom. I say that because ancient Israel was to be the established place of God's Kingdom on earth and that was also the place of their inheritance. When Jesus came He preached the "Gospel of the Kingdom," He said over and over, "The Kingdom of heaven is at hand." Notice that though many things Jesus taught were questioned by the people, they never questioned, Jesus' Kingdom message. The Jewish people had a Kingdom mindset. They were all desiring God's Kingdom to be established through them in the land of their inheritance.

After Jesus' resurrection, before His ascension, the disciples asked Him, *"...Lord, will You at this time restore the Kingdom to Israel?" (Acts 1:6, NKJV)*

What Jesus' followers didn't understand at that time, was that when Jesus instituted the New Covenant, through His body and blood, he expanded the availability of the Kingdom representation from the people of Israel and the place of Israel, to whosoever would come, wherever they were living. As each one of us walk in our inheritance, we are inviting the Kingdom of God to take up residency, or time and space on the earth, wherever we are. Kingdom = inheritance

So if we are called to help others obtain their inheritance, another way to say it is, we are to help them do their part in establishing the Kingdom of God on the earth. When we help one another we become the answer to Jesus prayer, let Your Kingdom come, Your will be done on earth as it is in heaven. When we help each other, it's a way of living out our faithfulness to God and His Kingdom cause. By partnering

116

with the expansion of God's Kingdom on the earth through one another, we are doing what Jesus said; *"But seek first the Kingdom of God and His righteousness, and all these things shall be added to you."(Matt. 6:33, NKJV)*

What I understand now, is that by not helping those to whom God has given us is a way of being unfaithful to Him. God isn't just in me, He's also in all who are believers in Jesus as Savior and Messiah. That is why God said through Moses, to the tribes who didn't want to help their brothers, your sin will find you out. Whether we don't help people because we are jealous, selfish, or apathetic, it's actually being unfaithful to God. It is sin in God's eyes, because it amounts to unfaithfulness to Him. Think about it, if the Kingdom reality is the best and we are unwilling to help those He has entrusted us to get there, we aren't being faithful to the One we claim we will do anything for.

I'm happy to say those two tribes heeded what Moses said to them. They responded,

> *...we will arm ourselves for battle and go ahead of the Israelites until we have brought them to their place...We will not return to our homes until each of the Israelites has received their inheritance... (Num. 32:17-19, NIV)*

The book of Joshua, records the battles the children of Israel fought in the early years of the conquest of the land. In all the details, God doesn't forget to mention these tribes' faithfulness to Him. After they fought for their brothers, they went back home to receive their promised inheritance.

> *So the LORD gave to Israel all the land of which He had sworn to give to their fathers, and they took possession of it and dwelt in it...Then Joshua called the Reubenites, the Gadites, and half the tribe of Manasseh, and*

117

said to them: "You have kept all that Moses the servant of the LORD commanded you, and have obeyed my voice in all that I commanded you. "You have not left your brethren these many days, up to this day, but have kept the charge of the commandments of the LORD your God. "And now the LORD your God has given rest to your brethren, as He promised them; now therefore, return and go to your tents and to the land of your possession, which Moses the servant of the LORD gave you on the other side of the Jordan.
(Josh.21:43 - 22:4, NKJV)

Chapter 7 – Questions

1. Can you think of a time, when another person's words gave you the encouragement and support you needed that helped you move forward?

2. How do you keep your ears attentive to the Holy Spirit so that you can know the "who" and "how" you are to help?

3. Why do you think Moses used such powerful language saying "Their sin would find them out," if they didn't cross over and fight alongside their brothers?

SESSION 7- VIDEO QUESTIONS

1. Has your relationship with your natural family made it easier or harder for you to feel close to your spiritual one?

2. Why do you think God wants you to do good "especially" to the household of faith?

3. What are some practical ways you can prefer other believers above yourself, specifically when it comes to helping them walk in their inheritance?

Chapter 8 – Israel and Your Inheritance

A PLACE

Perhaps one of the easiest observations to make about the land of Israel is that it's a place. That may not seem so mind-blowing at first thought, but I think it's telling about God and how He feels about His children. A place is defined as a portion of space designated to be used by someone. What parent would bring a newborn baby home that doesn't have a place prepared for them in the house? The scripture says that God has appointed a place for each person that they should live.

And He has made from one blood every nation of men to dwell on all the face of the earth, and has determined their preappointed times and the boundaries of their dwellings."
(Acts 17:26, NKJV)

When the Kingdom comes, I don't think Jesus will say, "Hey everybody just pick whatever place looks good to you." No! The God who knows every hair on your head also knows the place He has set aside for you, not only in His future Kingdom, but also while you're here on earth.

The places of our inheritance in this life are "designated spaces to be used by us." They include where we live, where we work, where we worship, and where we make our lives. This was just what the land of Israel was to be for the children of Israel. God told Moses:

*"Now therefore, go, lead the people to the
place of which I have spoken to you..."
(Ex. 32:34, NKJV)*

The reason God desires His children to have a place of their
own is so that we can be planted and be in peace. It's in the
places of our inheritance that God gives us authority for the
purpose of advancing and maintaining, God's causes in the
earth. God said to Joshua, *"Every place that the sole of your
foot will tread upon I have given you, as I said to Moses." (Josh.
1:3, NKJV)* Where your foot treads is another way of saying, in
the places I've called you to walk, I will give you authority.

Our authority is delegated authority, given by the Lord in
the places He sends us. It was to be within the bounds of the
land of Israel that the Hebrew people have the right to produce
fruit, defend it, and have dominion. In fact, God told the
children of Israel many times not to meddle with the land of
other people groups.

*And command the people, saying, "You are
about to pass through the territory of your
brethren, the descendants of Esau, who live in
Seir; and they will be afraid of you. Therefore
watch yourselves carefully. Do not meddle
with them, for I will not give you any of their
land, no, not so much as one footstep, because
I have given Mount Seir to Esau as a
possession." (Deut. 2:4-5, NKJV)*

*"And when you come near the people of
Ammon, do not harass them or meddle with
them, for I will not give you any of the land of
the people of Ammon as a possession, because
I have given it to the descendants of Lot as a
possession." (Deut. 2:19, NKJV)*

As unique as each one of us is, so will also be the places God
calls us to possess.

My brother Philip and his family moved to Vermont in 2006. After they had been gone a year, Chris got the idea he wanted to go visit them. Even though I hate long car rides we made plans and headed to Vermont for the weekend. When we arrived they were so happy to see us. Three of their kids are the same age as ours, so the playing commenced! The weekend was wonderful, we took the kids to the lake, explored the town of Burlington, and ate an amazing meal every night. To this day, Labor Day weekend 2007 was still one of the best trips we have ever had.

It's not unusual for Philip to joke around with me as most brothers do. While there that weekend, he kept teasing saying "Lynndey, when are you going to move to Vermont?" Every time he said it, I thought it was truly the stupidest thing he could say to me, which is what I think he intended it to be. He knew, I loved where I lived. I had everything I ever wanted in Virginia. There was absolutely no reason or desire for me to leave my home.

Our first visit to Vermont was so wonderful that they invited us to come back for New Years, saying we needed to see all the snow. We did and had another great trip, only this time it wasn't because of the peaceful lake and sun, but the beauty of the winter wonderland, of mountains and snow. While there the second time, Philip continued to tease me asking when we were going to move to Vermont. This time I gave him what I thought was an equally silly response. I told Philip, "I'll move to Vermont when God writes it in the sky for me." At this time in my life, I had no revelation of being surrendered to God in the area of where I lived, so the thought that God might be speaking to me didn't even cross my mind.

We went home and went on with our lives. About a month later, while vacuuming, I was recounting the silly back and forth Philip and I had about us moving to Vermont. I laughed to myself while repeating in my head my response to him, "When God writes it in the sky for me." As soon as I said those words in my head, I heard a loud voice speak from what sounded like it was behind me. The voice said, "**I will write it in the sky for you!**" I literally jumped and turned around to see who was there. In the second it took me to turn around to see who was there, I knew what happened. The Lord spoke to me. His voice wasn't audible, but it might as well have been. His words rang so loud in my head. It was a moment I'll never forget.

I kept the experience to myself for about two weeks. I knew Chris would be on board with moving a he was tired of his commute and loves adventure. I was right, as soon as I told him, he was ready to move. I was not! If it really was the Lord, He was going to have to do what He said and write it in the sky for me.

Chris started looking everywhere for the sign, while I kept my eyes low. Thirty years of my life had been down that driveway. I was in no rush to leave. A month or two passed, nothing was happening, and all I was doing was hoping God had forgotten what He said and wished that Chris would too.

At that time, Chris and I had season passes for historic Williamsburg, which was about two hours from our house. One Saturday, Chris got tickets for a Christian comedy show that was playing at the old playhouse there. We decided to take our two older kids who were eleven and seven at the time. The comedy show wasn't until the evening, so we also made plans to check out the museum there as we had never visited it before.

That afternoon, after making our way through the lower level of the museum we went up to the second floor. Chris walked into one of the rooms with a rotating exhibit while I was still looking at a display in the hallway. He entered the room for a minute, then ran back out into the hallway, grabbed my hand and said, "You have to see this!" He led me into a very large U shaped room where I saw ten large signs hanging from

124

the ceiling. They all said the same thing, "From Virginia to Vermont." My jaw dropped! The exhibit was colonial furniture made in Virginia, to be sold in Vermont. Chris, said, "It's the sign, it's the sign!" I couldn't disagree that the signs were very interesting in light of what was going on with us. Of all the rotating exhibits to walk into we had to walk in when it had those signs displayed! After the shock wore off, I nicely told Chris, "These signs are up high but they are NOT written in the sky." Chris, conceded, they weren't the sign, but we agreed they did mean something. The dinner conversation with our two kids afterwards was dominated by what it would be like if our family moved to Vermont.

After dinner, we went to the playhouse for the comedy show. The theater had about four-hundred seats that were first come first serve. We grabbed our seats and began to settle in. A large group came in right after us, taking the seats directly in front of us. As the theater was filling up, Chris leaned over to me and said, "Look at the guy directly in front of us, does his water bottle say Vermont?" I leaned up, glanced over his shoulder and there I saw it, a water bottle that had a picture of a field, a cow, and Vermont written across the sky. I couldn't believe it, first the ten signs and now this, all in the same night! This man presumably sat as randomly as we did in a four hundred person theater. Why did he have to have a water bottle with Vermont written in the sky? We got up and went to the concession stand to see if they were selling them. They weren't. The concession stand wasn't even open, making it even MORE random that he had that water bottle with Vermont written in the sky! I couldn't get out of it this time; Vermont was written in the sky. I am not a statistical expert; I didn't have to be to know in that moment that God was speaking and we were about to make the move from Virginia to Vermont.

A couple months passed by as Chris was looking for a job. Not many things were opening up, but he did get one interview with the local hospital. The position was for an IT job but the pay was significantly less than his current salary. He had two

125

phone interviews where they expressed their interest in hiring him. At that point, it seemed like the job was his to accept. All he had left was the third phone interview, for them to formally extend the position.

The day before this final phone call I was freaking out! All I had known my whole life was in Virginia! That whole day, I kept saying to myself, "I'm moving my entire life over a water bottle, am I crazy? This doesn't make any sense! What am I doing? This cannot be God!"

I went to go get my oil changed that day. With doubts consuming me, I took my seat in the waiting room of the shop. I kept repeating those questions over and over again in my head. To take my mind off of it, I picked up a magazine that was next to me. On the cover it said the ten best towns to live in the United States. In my desperation I said "Lord if you really want us to move to Vermont, it's going to be one of the top ten towns in the magazine." I opened to the article and South Burlington, right where Chris's job offer was, was on the list! UGH! I couldn't seem to get away from it. My drive home after all my errands that day was about twenty minutes. I literally cried the whole way home telling God, "I can't do it, I cannot move!" Once more I said, "If this is really you God, You will have to write it in the sky for me one more time, and it has to be today!"

As I pulled into the driveway I stopped to get our mail. In the mail that day was a big yellow envelope. As I walked into my living room, pretty much where I was standing when He told me He would write it in the sky for me, I opened the yellow envelope, curious to see what was inside. Everything began to move in slow-motion as I pulled out a full color picture of the Vermont sky over Lake Champlain with the words, **WELCOME TO VERMONT**... Immediately, all the doubt and anxiety of the day's thoughts stopped. Peace filled my heart. There was no more questioning it, God was calling us to this place. Thirty minutes after I asked the Lord, "Please write it in the sky for me one more time today!" He did, and there was nothing left to do but go to the place He was showing us.

The mysterious envelope came from a real estate agent we had never reached out to. This agent was married to the man Chris was interviewing with, and she took it upon herself to send us some information about Vermont. We moved to Vermont a few months later. We spent eight wonderful, hard, challenging, life changing years there. Our life in Vermont became not only part of our family's story, but a place of inheritance. We could never have imagined the spiritual growth and the wonderful things God had in store for us there. Why couldn't the things that happened to us in Vermont, happen in Virginia? I don't know, except I'm sure it's the same reason, the children of Israel couldn't stay in Egypt or the wilderness. They were called to go to the place of their inheritance, just like their father Abraham. It's in the places that God appoints for us in this life, that we find our inheritance in Him.

A PURPOSE

Every part of God's creation has a purpose. The trees, the ocean, the moon, even spiders, and snakes all have a purpose. As believers our purposes are multifaceted. While some are general in nature, like loving the Lord with all your heart, soul, mind, and strength, other purposes are as unique as each person. Our unique purposes are often found doing the things God has gifted us to do. For some, our purposes are the answers to society's problems or the causes that make our hearts come alive. As we mature in the Lord discovering and fulfilling our unique purposes becomes a source of joy like no other.

While it's easy for us to agree that we all have a purpose, I would like to suggest something about your purpose that you may have never thought of before. Our purposes will primarily

127

be discovered in the place of our inheritance. Place and purpose go hand in hand when it comes to your inheritance! The Father's declaration to Jesus, in Psalm 2 shows this idea, that place and purpose go hand in.

> *I will proclaim the LORD's decree: He said*
> *to me, "You are my son; today I have become*
> *your father. Ask me, and **I will make the***
> ***nations your inheritance**, the ends of the earth*
> *your possession." (Psalm 2:7-8, NIV)*

Jesus had to come to the place of His inheritance to fulfill His purpose. Only as a man with His feet on the ground could Jesus preach the gospel of the Kingdom and fulfill the Father's promise to the Jewish people to send the Messiah. Only as the sinless man and son of David, could Jesus claim the throne of Israel, and Ruler of the nations.

When Jesus finished that purpose, He was called back to heaven to fulfill the role of the great High Priest of heaven. For now, He remains at the Father's right hand making intercession for the saints. Wherever Jesus is, He fulfills the purpose God has for Him in that place.

Though we were actively involved in a local house of prayer, as soon as we moved to Vermont, a year went by and we were still looking for a church family. A friend suggested a church a couple miles from our new house. We checked it out the following Sunday. It seemed like everyone there was friendly but most importantly we felt the Holy Spirit's presence during the service, so we began attending.

Our second Sunday there, the pastor announced a ladies night with a special guest speaker the following Sunday night. When he announced the gathering the Holy Spirit whispered to me, "You should go." The following Sunday came around and as we had just moved into our home, I had been unpacking all day. As evening came, I really didn't feel like going anywhere. I was tired and just wanted to sit on the couch for the rest of the night. As I was talking myself out of going, I felt the Lord ask me if I was going to obey Him. I yielded to the Holy Spirit, ran out of the house a little disheveled, arriving moments before it began.

That church had a pretty big sanctuary but there were only about ten ladies in attendance. I remember feeling bad for the speaker as she began since the attendance was so low. She didn't seem to mind. She began her message with passion and enthusiasm. I hate to admit it, but about five minutes into the message, I remember thinking, "I've heard all this before.... I don't know why I'm here; this is a waste of my time." After about five minutes of those thoughts and feelings rolling around in my head, the speaker abruptly stopped her message. She said to everyone, "I have to stop, because there is a spirit here, telling people they don't know why they are here, they have heard all this before, this is a waste of their time!" I sat up really straight. I was completely shocked! She just quoted my EXACT thoughts! She proceeded to command the distracting spirit to leave and prayed that the Lord's voice would be heard instead.

The whole atmosphere changed, it was like heaven opened up and I was its receptacle. Suddenly, everything she said was applicable to my life. Her message was on the abundance of God's Kingdom. She contrasted the world's economy with God's economy. In the world's economy everything is wasting away, everything is running out. The Kingdom's economy is the opposite of the world's. In God's economy, there is more than enough of every resource to do all that God desires us to do. She ended the night with a powerful exhortation to dream with God. She instructed us to go home and quiet our minds and open our hearts. She said, "With your heart wide open tell God what you would like to do for Him." She urged us to not put off what we desire to do for God for five or ten years, but to begin to put our hands to the plow now, knowing we are working in the Kingdom economy of more than enough.

I couldn't wait to go home and go to sleep so I could wake up the next morning and spend time with God. I knew her words were the Lord's to me, after all, He had gone through great lengths to get me there and to pay attention to the word that night. I got up early the next morning, and began to meditate on the message and ask myself the question, "What would I like to do for God in this life?" I could feel God's nearness as I began to pray. As my heart and mind were opened I began to think over the transformation God had done in my life over the last four years.

Prior to those last four years, my faith in Jesus was sincere, but my personal relationship with God was greatly lacking. So when the enemy came to trip me up in my late twenties, he was much smarter than me. For a season I went far away from God. Neither Chris nor I were where we wanted to be in life, so we searched high and low to find a church to make our home. We didn't know how to fix our lives, but we knew Jesus was the answer. After attending church again for a year, with life not really getting any better, our pastor had a man, Joseph get up and share his testimony. He shared that when he became a serious student of the scriptures that his whole life dramatically changed. The Holy Spirit grabbed my heart in that moment, and I said to myself, "I've tried everything else; I think I'll try reading the Bible!

Every time I think about it now I laugh. How silly is it for someone who has been in the church most of their life to say they will try reading the Bible? Yet since then I've discovered, it's actually the state of most believers. At that time, in our lives, Chris was leaving for work at 4:15 in the morning, so I got up with him each day and had about an hour and a half with God before the kids got up. What, Joseph, testified in church that day became true for me too. When I began to know God through His word, everything changed! Through His word, God taught me how to live and how to commune with Him. In His word I found hope, I found healing, I found forgiveness. In God's word, I found the way to live a life free from the strongholds of sin. In His word I found the answers to the questions I had for everyday life. I found enjoyment, I found freedom, I found excitement! As I sat in my chair four years later dreaming with God, that was all I could think about. The same experience I had, I wanted to help others have. For all the other believers out there who were overwhelmed by the scriptures or thought it was too much to learn or too hard to understand, I wanted to show them the same treasure I found. That was the answer to the question "What would you do for God?" With tears running down my face I very simply said to the Lord, "I want to teach Your word to others, so they can find what I have found in You."

That was the moment I consider receiving my "calling or my purpose" from God. After that, through just following Him and telling others the dream that was in my heart, God has given me many opportunities to teach His word. When you are doing something God has purposed you to do, the Holy Spirit will anoint and empower you to accomplish it. When you are doing what you are purposed to do, you're alive like at no other time, you're walking in your inheritance!

THREE CAUTIONS

Though seeking out the purposes God has for you in life are important, three cautions come to mind. The first being, that I have seen some get so focused on finding their purpose, or fulfilling their destiny, that it becomes an obsession. With any obsession, it can become paralyzing, stopping you from enjoying each day and season of life. We are called to live a life of peace, knowing that finding meaning will come as we follow God each day.

The second caution I have is this, we shouldn't get so focused on doing one thing that we don't make allowances for God's purposes to express themselves differently in different seasons. Learning to move with the Spirit and the transitions our lives are made up of, will help us not get caught up in feeling the need to express our purpose in one way for the rest of our lives. Many who think they need to do that end up disappointed and disillusioned. Just think about people like David, Moses, and even Jesus. There were different seasons in their lives, and all of them were unto God's purposes. God needed Moses to grow up in Pharaoh's house, but He also wanted him to experience the back side of the desert for forty years before he was called to be the nation's deliverer. In all those seasons, God had a purpose. Though David was anointed king, he had to spend thirteen years running for his life before he took the throne. Jesus, spent the first thirty years of his life hanging out with his earthly family before He began His ministry. Every season has a purpose when we surrender it to God.

My last caution is this, our identity is not dependent on our purpose. Once some discover purpose, the tendency is to link identity and purpose together. I made that mistake myself as I began to teach. I began finding my identity in teaching instead of just resting in my identity as His child. We must always remember there is no chart in heaven that needs to be filled in with the things you "do" that will make God love you more. He loves and values you just because you are His child, period. Our purpose consists of the things we will do, our identity is the essence of who we are.

God told the nation of Israel, it wasn't for anything they had done that He loved them, He just loved them. "*The LORD did not set His love on you nor choose you because you were more in number than any other people, for you were the least of all peoples.*" (*Deut. 7:7-8, NIV*) They weren't the most numerous nation, they hadn't done anything special, yet He chose to set His love upon them. Even in their mistakes, even in their failures, He loved them. Why? Because they are His people. It's the same for all who are in the family of God. He loves you, just because He loves you.

Some of the purposes of the nation of Israel include:

1. God purposed them to be a *"special treasure to Him above all people."* Ex. 19:5

2. They were to be *"a kingdom of priests and a holy nation"* Ex.19:6

3. They were to be the nation where the temple would be built, for God to dwell with man. *"He shall build a house for my name"* 2 Sam. 7:13

4. The people among who He would dwell, *"And let them make me a sanctuary; that I may dwell among them"* Ex. 25:8

5. They were to carry the word of God to the world, *"because that unto them were committed the oracles of God"* Rom.3:2

6. Through their family would come the Messiah and Savior of the world would come, *"and all people on earth will be blessed through you"* Gen.12:3

7. Their story was to be an example to the church. *1Cor.10*

8. Through the early disciples of Jesus, the church was birthed and the Holy Spirit came. *Acts 2*

A PEOPLE

God loves people! I once again want to remind you as I'm urging you to possess your inheritances, that possessing our inheritance isn't mainly about us. It's about the Kingdom and the people God longs to be a part of it! By walking in the places and purposes of your inheritance, you will become a blessing to people.

It was no different for the children of Israel, their lives and their story, their inheritance was not only for themselves but for someone else. And that someone is actually the whole rest of the world, the Gentiles.

THEIR LIVES BECAME OUR EXAMPLES

The most popular book of all time, the Bible, contains the stories of the family of Abraham. The scripture pens the accounts of the nation's highest highs and lowest lows. Their lives and stories were written for us to benefit from!

I have a Jewish friend who asked me one time, "Would you like your entire family's history to be written in a book for the whole world to read?" My answer is "No!" With their most intimate details exposed for the world to read, we can learn how God relates to mankind through His covenant people, Israel. The accounts of the Hebrews lives are a treasured gift to the world. I see through their lives, that I like them, could never come to the measure of holiness required to be in a relationship with a Holy God. Instead what I need is the same thing they needed, a God who would save me.

Not only were their stories written for us, their lives also became the conduit of blessing to the entire world. God promised to Abraham. *"And through your descendants all the nations of the earth will be blessed" (Gen 22:18, NLT)*

The word blessed, can mean to kneel down and give someone something. Through the people of Israel, God, knelt down to the earth, in the person of Jesus. God blessed the world with what it desperately needed, a way to get back into relationship with Him. I pray the church never forgets, the nation of Israel gave birth to the Messiah, Savior of the world.

It was Jesus Hebrew disciples that He left to spread the message of who He is to the known world. Jesus told His disciples that to them was given the ability to know the mysteries of the Kingdom. It was the apostles that carried the weight of leadership in the early church, to which most of them gave their lives. Very specifically God called one Hebrew man, Saul, a Pharisee by upbringing, to become the apostle to the Gentile church. God showed Paul a secret long held in His heart that He would open up salvation to the Gentiles.

> *By which when you read , you may understand my knowledge in the mystery of Christ, which in other ages was not made known to the sons of men, as it has now been revealed by the Spirit to His holy apostles and prophets: that the Gentiles should be fellow heirs, of the same body ,and partakers of His promise in Christ through the gospel...To me, who am less than the least of all the saints, this grace was given, that I should preach among the Gentiles the unsearchable riches of Christ.(Eph. 3:4-8, NKJV)*

As a Gentile, I am thankful that a Jewish man named Paul didn't let anything stop him from going to the places of his inheritance, from planting churches, and fulfilling God's call on his life, which became a blessing for the entire Gentile world.

GOD IS FAITHFUL

God is not finished with the nation of Israel yet, there is still more to their inheritance yet to be seen. Some people call the nation, God's prophetic time piece. The prophecies of the Bible concerning the nation of Israel are being fulfilled right now in this generation. One of the biggest prophecies being that they are back in the land of their inheritance! After the Holocaust, the land of Israel was once again set apart for the Jewish people in 1948. Since then, the Jewish people have been flocking back to the land of their inheritance. They are fulfilling many of the Old Testament prophecies, that God would call them out of the four corners of the earth to return to their land. No other nation in the history of the world, has been out of their homeland to return and take possession once again after 2,000 years. No other nation has come back to their land and spoke the same language, and conserved so much of their culture, like they have. And all this was foretold in the scriptures by God through His prophets.

The nation of Israel is truly a testimony to the faithfulness of God. It's too much to say in this segment, but even though things may look tough again in the future for the nation, God has a plan. You can be sure of this, there is something powerful that happens when the people of God are living in the place of their inheritance that causes them to fulfill the purposes of God, that will affect a people. As a nation, that journey is still unfolding today for the Hebrew people. As a Gentile, I am thankful for the people of Israel, and can't wait to see the fullness of their inheritance come at the end of the age. Paul said if their turning away meant riches for the world, what will it mean when their fullness comes?

> *Now if their fall is riches for the world, and their failure riches for the Gentiles, **how much more their fullness!** (Rom. 11:12, NKJV)*

A PLACE, A PURPOSE, AND A PEOPLE

I have been talking about the part of your inheritance I believe will be found in this life, that includes a place a purpose and a people, it's exciting to note that our eternal inheritance will also include those three things as well. Jesus said in *John 14:2, "I go to prepare a place for you."* One day, God will create a new heaven and a new earth as Revelation 21 tells us. As the redeemed, we will inherit a literal place inside God's eternal Kingdom.

In Matthew 25, when Jesus was describing the Kingdom of heaven, He said the faithful servant would be made ruler over many things. I believe this is just a glimpse into the eternal Kingdom. Based on our faithfulness in this life to do with what we have been given, God will have assignments, positions, and many things for us to accomplish in His Kingdom. I promise you we won't be bored! We won't be aimlessly floating around on clouds. We will have purposes to fulfill in the next age, just like in this one.

The people that will be affected in the next age, by us possessing our inheritance in the eternal Kingdom is us and God. The following verse, says what God plans to do with us for eternity. He wants to show us the exceeding riches of His grace and kindness He made available to us through Jesus.

> *...that in the ages to come He might show*
> *the exceeding riches of His grace in His*
> *kindness toward us in Christ Jesus.*
> *(Eph. 2:7, NKJV)*

I picture the above verse going something like this: As we enter the age of eternity and all our inheritances have all been given out, now it's time for the Father to receive His. He gathers His children from across all time and has us stand with our backs to Him as He gazes out in the new heavens and the new earth. Standing behind us, He then declares to all creation, "Look at my children. They chose Me, though they never saw Me! They trusted Me above all else, and now I have brought them to Myself through the Messiah to be with me forever."

As we receive the fullness of our inheritance God will receive the fullness of His, His glory in our redemption. The redeemed will be an eternal display of the goodness and greatness of our God. His glory will be revealed in us. That is truly mind blowing! May we continually honor our God, by being those who pursue our inheritance found in places, purpose and people.

1. Why do you think it's important to God for you to go to the places He calls you to? What is it He can do with you in those places that He can't do with you other places?

2. Our purposes sometimes change and develop from season to season during our lives. What are some of the main purposes that God is calling you to walk in, in the season of life you are in now?

3. What people group do you especially feel drawn toward, to help? How do you see yourself helping them?

SESSION 8 – VIDEO QUESTIONS

1. Has there been a time that you have surrendered to God, the decision to go to a "place?"

2. What situation in your life is God using to deepen your trust in Him at this time?

3. What situation is there in your life currently that is inviting you to humble yourself?

Chapter 9 – Naboth's Vineyard

T ucked in the Old Testament is the account of a man from the tribe of Issachar, named Naboth. As many of the seemingly insignificant narratives in the scriptures do, this story displays a powerful truth concerning your inheritance. You just have to look a little deeper to see it!

Naboth lived in a tumultuous time in Israel, under the reign of King Ahab and his wife Jezebel. King Ahab had the distinct honor of being one of the worst kings in Israel's history! *"Ahab did more to provoke the LORD God of Israel to anger than all the kings of Israel that were before him." (1 Kings 16:33, NKJV)* Jezebel wasn't any better, her acts were so vile that her name has become synonymous for evil women throughout history since her reign of terror.

Together from the highest position in the land, Ahab and Jezebel waged war against God and anyone who remained faithful to Him. They built idols for the people to worship and murdered anyone that opposed them, including many of God's prophets.

THE VALLEY OF JEZREEL

When the children of Israel originally entered the land four hundred years earlier, the land was divided first by tribe, and then again by individual families. As part of their inheritance, Naboth's family was given the land of Jezreel. Because the water from Mt. Hermon floods the valley yearly depositing rich minerals into the soil, the valley of Jezreel has always been known as an extremely fertile and desirable place. It was from this same valley that the twelve Israelite spies brought back huge grapes to show just how awesome the land God was giving them was. At that time they called is Eschol.

The Jezreel valley has also been the location of many famous battles. Deborah and Barak fought the Canaanites there. Gideon defeated the Midianites with his army of three hundred there. Kings Saul, Ahaziah, and Josiah were all injured or killed in the valley fighting in Israel's wars. Even in recent history, Napoleon fought the Turks there. And a little later on, Britain defended Israel from the Turks, all in this same valley!

This area is well known to many because of all the battles fought there, but I dare say the battle this valley is most well-known for is a battle that is yet to come. The battle of Armageddon. The Jezreel valley, is also known as Megiddo, Megiddo is the tell (archaeological mound) overlooking the valley. It will be from this same place that Jesus will come to fight the last battle for the earth as told in Revelation 16. For all this history and what is yet to come, the valley of Jezreel is symbolic of the struggle God's people have had against evil, and the ultimate victory of God against His enemies.

NABOTH, THE JEZREELITE

In 1 Kings 21 there is recorded yet another event surrounding this valley that once again symbolizes the struggle between man and our enemy, over our inheritance! Seemingly minding his own business, Naboth the Jezreelite gets a visit to his vineyard one day from the King of Israel. King Ahab, had a request for Naboth:

> *"Let me have your vineyard to use for a vegetable garden, since it is close to my palace. In exchange I will give you a better vineyard or, if you prefer, I will pay you whatever it is worth.*

But Naboth replied, "The LORD forbid that
I should give you the inheritance of my
ancestors."

So Ahab went home, sullen and angry
because Naboth the Jezreelite had said, "I will
not give you the inheritance of my ancestors."
He lay on his bed sulking and refused to eat.
(1 Kings 21:2-4, NIV)

Ahab, came home crying like a baby, but his wife Jezebel
had a different response.

His wife Jezebel came in and asked him,
"Why are you so sullen? Why won't you eat?"

He answered her, "Because I said to
Naboth the Jezreelite, 'Sell me your vineyard;
or if you prefer, I will give you another
vineyard in its place.' But he said, 'I will not
give you my vineyard.'"

Jezebel his wife said, "Is this how you act
as king over Israel? Get up and eat! Cheer up.
I'll get you the vineyard of Naboth the
Jezreelite."
(1 Kings 21:5-7, NIV)

Jezebel set a plan in motion. She sent letters to the elders of
Naboth's city and told them to host a special dinner. At that
dinner, she instructed them to seat Naboth at the place of
honor while sitting two men willing to lie for the queen next to
him. During the dinner the men on either side were instructed
by, Jezebel, to stand up and accuse Naboth of blaspheming God
and the king, the penalty for which is being stoned to death.

Then two scoundrels came and sat opposite
him and brought charges against Naboth
before the people, saying, "Naboth has cursed

both God and the king." So they took him
outside the city and stoned him to death.
(1 Kings 21:13, NIV)

As soon as Jezebel heard that Naboth had been stoned to death, she said to Ahab:

*"Get up and **take possession (yarash)** of the*
vineyard of Naboth the Jezreelite that he
refused to sell you. He is no longer alive, but
dead." When Ahab heard that Naboth was
*dead, he got up and went down to **take***
***possession (yarash)** of Naboth's vineyard.*
(1 Kings 21:15-16, NIV)

Jezebel got what she wanted, Naboth's inheritance!

THERE'S A PATTERN

Think about the similarities between Naboth's story and what happened in the Garden of Eden. God, appointed Naboth's family a portion of land. Within that land, they had the responsibility to tend it, to keep it, and to exercise authority over it. By tending and keeping his God-given inheritance, Naboth and his family had a place they could grow and thrive for generations to come. It was to be a place of peace and security, a place they could have fellowship with God. But an enemy came along wanting what God gave to Naboth. By use of trickery and deceit, that which was meant to give Naboth life was taken from him. The main difference between Naboth and Adam was, Naboth did not give over to the enemy what God had given to him, it was taken from him, quite literally over his dead body!

Just like Satan wanted to take what God gave to Adam and Naboth, he wants to yarash, or take possession of all that God has for you. He wants to yarash the place of authority God has given to you. He wants to yarash, the places God has for you to

144

tend and keep, the places meant for you to enjoy God's fellowship. And he will use the same methods of twisting the truth, lies, and accusations against you and God, to get it if he can!

Naboth represents a believer who no matter the cost is following after God. Though, Naboth, doesn't look like a winner in this story, he was. Naboth was willing to protect with his life what God had given him. I believe because of His faithfulness to the Lord, the reward of his inheritance in the next life will be far greater than what he lost. Although there isn't much written about Naboth, he possessed three valuable qualities we should all possess when it comes to defending our inheritance in this life from the schemes of the adversary.

OVERCOMING THE IDOL OF CONVENIENCE

*Ahab said to Naboth, "Let me have your vineyard to use for a vegetable garden, **since it is close to my palace.** In exchange I will give you a better vineyard or, if you prefer, I will pay you whatever it is worth."*
(1 Kings 21:2, NIV)

Ahab, wanted, Naboth's vineyard because it was next to his. The proposed deal was one of convenience. Ahab's offer to Naboth represents the same deal the world extends to you and I every day, do what is convenient, even when it comes to following God. One definition of convenient is, "involving little or no trouble, or effort." Wouldn't you agree, this is the motto of the world? Do the thing that causes you the least amount of effort, do whatever is easiest for you.

Pursuing and maintaining what God has for you in this life will require effort. Like we've seen with the children of Israel, it's more than likely that a good portion of the inheritance God has for you will not conveniently fall into your lap. The whole

145

idea surrounding the Hebrew word yarash is there will be things God wants for you that you will have to get up and go after. Jesus said, seek and you will find, knock and the door will be opened to you. These commands take action.

You may wonder why God requires any effort on our part. After all our relationship with God isn't based on our work, so why then do we have to put forth effort, to obtain that which He desires to give to us? Can't all that He desires to give us just drop into our laps? While our relationship with God is not works based, it is based on love. Therefore the question is NOT what are you willing to do to get what God has for you, but, what will you do because of love?

Remember when you were young and you could stay up all night talking on the phone to your boyfriend or girlfriend? Remember, when driving forty-five minutes each way to see them was nothing? Remember the early days of love? Or remember, when you got up all night with your newborn baby? Remember, when you got up early to fix your spouse's coffee and kiss them goodbye before work? Can you look back in life and see the things love has compelled you to do?

PUTTING IN THE EFFORT

To be close to someone, you have to spend time with them, and to be really close to them, one-on-one time. It's no different with our relationship with God. One of the things that hinders believers most from walking in the freedom and power we have access to is the lack of effort we put into spending time with God. If we trade that effort for what comes easy or convenient, we will end up with a very shallow relationship with our Heavenly Father, one that will not be able to sustain us through the storms of life.

With four kids and a husband who works from home, the only alone time I have to spend time with God is BEFORE they

146

all get up! For me, the biggest convenience I've had to give up to pursue a relationship with the Lord is that extra hour of sleep in the morning. When the alarm goes off at 5:45 am it takes effort to get out of that bed! For others it may be turning the TV off an hour earlier each night. It may be giving up going to lunch with your co-workers so you can eat alone while talking to God in the car. No matter the specific time our schedule allows us to seek God, the truth is it will never really be convenient.

A few years ago, Chris and I bought a fixer-upper. We were on a tight deadline and had a lot of work to do to get the house complete in time. We were physically working twelve hours a day for a couple weeks during the final push to have the house ready. Between being physically exhausted and unpacking for weeks, I got completely out of my routine of waking up early to spend time with God. Next thing you know, three months of very little alone time with God went by. I guess Chris was noticing a difference in my general attitude and countenance. One evening, I must have been displaying a really bad attitude, when Chris looked at me and said, "You are waking up tomorrow to spend time with Jesus!" He grabbed my phone and set my alarm for 5:30am. He reminded me what I knew but wasn't walking in for those three months. It takes effort on our part to seek God and by extension what He has for us. A little less sleep was needed in my life, so I could have a lot more God! This isn't an awe inspiring revelation, that you need to spend time with God, I'm sure you've heard it before. But I promise you, if you will consistently spend time with the Creator of the Universe, you will live a life filled with awe and wonder at Him.

God isn't looking for workers, who are striving for an inheritance, but He is looking for whole-hearted lovers! The idol of convenience will always have its hand stretched out to you, but don't let it trick you into giving away that which God has reserved for you! It will be those whose devotion for Him is worth putting in effort to do what isn't easy who will get that which is priceless. He is looking for those who think their inheritance in Him is worth saying no to what's easy, to lay hold of what is good. It would have been easy for Naboth to give Ahab that vineyard. But Naboth was not willing to do what was convenient when it came to giving up his inheritance.

BOLDNESS

The wicked flee when no one pursues, but the righteous are bold as a lion.
(Prov. 28:1, NKJV)

My seventeen year old son Luke often says about someone he is impressed with, "That's a bold move!" It was a bold move for Naboth to say no to the king of Israel. Especially knowing that saying no to him was also saying no to Jezebel! Jezebel was known for being ruthless when people crossed her. Even the prophet Elijah ran scared at her threats.

Boldness is defined as a willingness to take risks and act innovatively. It means going beyond the usual limits of conventional thought or action. When you take risks, when you do something that is outside of conventional thinking, when you go beyond what seems doable, it's then that your walking in faith.

Bold faith is always on the menu when it comes to following God. Just read the Bible. God took a group of ex-slaves from Egypt and told them to go to war against well-armed, well trained giants. God told Gideon to fight an army of around 135,000 Midanites with an army of 300! God told Mary, a virgin that she was pregnant, and it's going to be ok. God told Abraham, a man with not one child, you will be a father of nations. David, who was probably under 6 feet tall went out to fight a man 9 feet tall, only armed with 5 rocks. Turn to most any page in the Bible and you will see everyday people making bold moves for God.

My own journey to possess my inheritance has taken a large amount of boldness. When people see my standing in front of large crowds speaking, people think I am naturally a bold person. The truth is I'm not. But to become the person that God has called me to be, I've had to push past what is comfortable, knowing that since God is with me, I don't have to worry about only doing what comes natural to me. Instead I rely on the Spirit of God living in me.

> *By his divine power, God has given us everything we need for living a godly life. We have received all of this by coming to know him, the one who called us to himself by means of his marvelous glory and excellence.*
> *(2 Pet. 1:3, NKJV)*

It is God who makes us strong, it's Him who makes us brave, it's Him who gives us the inner resolve to do what He has called us to do. To claim the fullness of our inheritance in this life will require us to take what seem like risks and go beyond those things that have limited us in the past. In plain talk, you will have to get out of your comfort zone to claim the inheritance God has for you, I guarantee it!

NOT COMPROMISING ON GOD'S WORD

> *Ahab said to Naboth, "Let me have your vineyard to use for a vegetable garden, since it is close to my palace. In exchange I will give you a better vineyard or, if you prefer, I will pay you whatever it is worth."*
>
> *But Naboth replied, "**The LORD forbid that I should give you the inheritance of my ancestors**." (1 Kings 21:2-3, NIV)*

When you first read this you may think to yourself, what's the big deal, why wouldn't Naboth sell Ahab this vineyard? Ahab offered to pay him for it. He also offered to give him one better. It seems fair. It makes sense right? This is the temptation of the world, do things that make sense in our minds, even if they go against God's word.

The land that Naboth owned was given to his family when the children of Israel entered the land over four hundred years earlier. Part of the Jezreel valley was given to Naboth's family the tribe of Issachar.

The fourth lot came out for Issachar
according to its clans. Their territory included:

Jezreel...These towns and their villages
were the inheritance of the tribe of Issachar,
according to its clans. (Josh. 19:17-23, NIV)

Before the children of Israel entered the land, God had a few specific instructions as to what they could and could not do regarding their inherited land. They were not to sell or give away their inherited land to anyone outside of their specific tribe, doing so would have made the inheritance of the tribes fluctuate. God wanted each tribe to have what He originally gave to them, nothing more, nothing less. In other words, Naboth could have sold it to another person from the tribe of Isaachar but not to Ahab, as he was from the tribe of Ephraim.

No inheritance in Israel is to pass from one
tribe to another, for every Israelite shall keep
the tribal inheritance of their ancestors.
(Num. 36:7, NIV)

Naboth, said the Lord forbid that I give my inheritance to you, because the Lord really did forbid it. Even though it would have been easy for Naboth to give or sell his vineyard to Ahab it would have been against God's word.

We as believers must realize to live a life of holiness, our lives must look different than the world's. The world has said, it makes no sense to marry someone before you have lived with them or been intimate with them. How will you know if you get along? The world has said, it makes no sense to discipline your children, instead reason with them. The world has said, it doesn't make sense to give a tenth of your income to God, that makes you have less. The world has said, do whatever feels good, whatever feels right to you, follow your truth. But living for God means following a standard so much higher than our own natural minds, it means following God at His word. Jesus said, *"But why do you call Me 'Lord, Lord,' and not do the things which I say? (Luke 6:46, NKJV)*

As we come closer and closer to the end of the age, God's word, will become more and more intolerable for the world. But for those who love the Lord, His word will become more and more precious. God's word is life, His word is power, in His word is found everything that we need to direct our daily lives. As the gap between God's word and the way of the world increases, we must ask ourselves, will we magnify the word of God even when the world calls it evil? Will His word be our standard even when obeying it is not convenient? And when the word of God requires us to take a bold stance, what will we do?

I pray that we can be like Naboth. Because even though he gave his life, he held in the highest esteem the inheritance granted to him by God. When the temptation of doing what was easy came his way, he did not waver giving into the idol of convenience. Instead Naboth stood boldly by God's word. In order to walk in the measure of authority God has granted to us in this life, and our inheritance, we MUST not give it up for anything, just like Naboth.

AHAB

So many times in the scriptures we see the Israelites having to defend themselves from the surrounding people groups. But Naboth's enemy was not an outsider, he was a fellow Israelite. Though Ahab, should have been a friend, he symbolizes a foolish person who by connecting himself to Jezebel, ended up joining Satan's cause of stealing inheritance from God's people.

> *And it came to pass, as if it had been a light thing for him to walk in the sins of Jeroboam the son of Nebat, that he took to wife Jezebel the daughter of Ethbaal king of the Sidonians, and went and served Baal, and worshipped him. (1 Kings 16:31, NKJV)*

As the Creator of marriage, God knows the power of influence that comes from the one you join yourself to. God commanded the children of Israel not to marry foreign women. Ahab, decided he didn't need to follow God's word and married a foreign woman anyway. Ahab's life is just another testimony that God knows what He is talking about! It matters who your connected to!

> *Don't be fooled, bad friends will ruin good habits. (1 Cor. 15:33, ERV)*

> *Do not be **unequally yoked** together with unbelievers. For what fellowship has righteousness with lawlessness? And what communion has light with darkness? (2 Cor. 6:14, NKJV)*

The world's systems are run by Satan, he is the prince and the power of the air. Too many believers have immersed themselves so far into the culture in an effort to be relevant, that they look more like Ahab and less like Naboth. The valid and burning question in the church has become, how are we to operate as ambassadors to the world if we don't connect with them? And the answer is found in the phrase unequally yoked.

When a yoke is placed on two animals' necks, it's for the purpose of them walking side by side in harmony so as to plow the field quickly and evenly. They must go to the same place, at the same speed and in the same rhythm. We all need to realize that in the spirit realm, we will be yoked to whoever we marry, to who our good friends are, to the YouTube videos we watch regularly, and in the music we listen to. We must periodically ask ourselves, are all my yokes even? If they aren't we may have some de-yoking to do, in order to not be swayed by the enemy, like Ahab so easily was.

Yes, we should talk to non-believers. If we didn't, how would they ever hear the good news Jesus saves? From Ahab's life, we need to learn that the boundary lines must be firm. As we wade the waters of relevancy, we must always be on guard asking ourselves, am I influencing the world or is it influencing me? We are to extend a hand to non-believers, bringing them the life of God so that they can be made whole. Our call is to pull them out, not join them!

> *Now therefore, do not give your daughters*
> *as wives for their sons, nor take their*
> *daughters to your sons; and never seek their*
> *peace or prosperity, that you may be strong*
> *and eat the good of the land, and leave it as an*
> *inheritance to your children forever."*
> *(Ezra 9:12, NKJV)*

God says if you separate yourself from the world you will remain in your inheritance, as well as your children. Though the world is constantly inviting us to join them, we must instead invite them to join us. If we choose to instead link up with the world, we shouldn't kid ourselves, we are really joining our enemy. James said, *"Do you not know that friendship with the world is enmity with God? Whoever therefore wants be a friend of the world makes himself an enemy of God. (James 4:4, NKJV)* May we never be like Ahab, full of compromise, influenced by the world, hurting God's people, and stealing inheritances.

JEZEBEL = SATAN

It will be no surprise to you for me to say, Jezebel, represents Satan and his desires for you and me. Jesus said, Satan was a thief and a murderer from the beginning. Like Satan, Jezebel lied, murdered, and stole from Naboth. Her desire was driven by envy and pride, all the same things that motivate Satan, the adversary against God's beloved, you and I.

> *...He (Satan) was a murderer from the beginning, not holding to the truth, for there is no truth in him. When he lies, he speaks his native language, for he is a liar and the father of lies. (John 8:44, NIV)*

When you were saved, Satan lost round one. His first aim being that you never come to eternal salvation. After your salvation, the battle he wages against you, is over your inheritance in this life.

As I shared at the beginning of this chapter, the Jezreel Valley has always been known for its abundance and fruitfulness. In fact, all the land of Israel was known for its bountifulness. This is why God wanted it for His children and why Satan did not. So too within your inheritance God has given you many fertile fields in which you may plant what I call, Kingdom seeds. Just like Naboth was cultivating his vineyard, we are called to cultivate the things that He has

154

given us. What makes Satan so afraid of you possessing your inheritance is the fruitfulness found within it!

Within your inheritance you are to grow spiritual food. This spiritual food is not only for you, but for those around you. It's through spiritual food that the people in the Kingdom of God grow and become strong. The health of a people group is found in the health and bounty of their crops.

Inheritance not only equals Kingdom, it equals healthy believers, being fed spiritual food! Jesus said *"Who then is a faithful and wise servant, whom his master made ruler over his household, **to give them food in due season?"** (Matt. 24:45, NKJV)* A faithful and wise servant will be found feeding those around them! This is the purpose of the thirty, sixty, and hundredfold harvest Jesus talked about in the parable of the seed.

This is why Satan DOES NOT WANT you to have that harvest, it's why he doesn't want you in your inheritance. That's why his desire is to try and trick or steal it from you like he did in the garden of Eden or like Jezebel did to Naboth. It's in the fertile fields of your inheritance that a crop grows that does damage to the Kingdom of darkness while simultaneously building up the Kingdom of God.

You may say all that sounds nice, but this account is not very encouraging, after all Naboth died in the end. It kinda looked like Satan won through Jezebel. But here is where we have an opportunity to have the long vision or true vision. There will always be times it seems like Satan is winning. But we must remember that no matter what it looks like on the earth, Jesus has already won.

The name Jezreel means God has sown. Because we are a spiritual people sowing spiritual seed, no matter what it looks like in the here and now, at the end of the age, all Kingdom seeds we have sown through God in this life, will be brought to

Kingdom harvest. In Hebrews 11, the writer acknowledges that Sarah and Abraham to whom God promised such a grand inheritance, never got to see the promises with their natural eyes. But that in their lives, they sowed seeds of faithfulness as they looked to the place where the fullness of the inheritance awaits, with God at the end of the age.

These all died in faith not having received the promises, but having seen them afar off were assured of them, embraced them and confessed that they were strangers and pilgrims on the earth for those who say such things declare plainly that they seek a homeland. And truly if they had called to mins that country from which they had come out, they would have had the opportunity to return, But now they desire a better, that it, a heavenly country. Therefore God is not ashamed to be called their God, for He has prepared a city for them.
(Heb. 11:13-16, NKJV)

I don't think it's any coincidence that the same place that was stolen from Naboth, will be the same place Jesus faces the armies of the world in the last battle. Remember, the Jezreel Valley is also known as the Valley of Megiddo, or Armageddon. What we have sown in the earth, through God will last beyond this natural life! At the end of the age when Jesus returns God will make all things right, no matter how they may appear in the natural in this age. Like God told the prophet Daniel, *"But you, go your way till the end; for you shall rest, and will arise to your inheritance at the end of the days."* (Dan. 12:13, NKJV)

As the Kingdom Age dawns, it will be like a time of Jubilee, where all that belongs to us including that which has been stolen will be restored. Until that day, may we be faithful like Naboth to cultivate all that God has given us in this life, trusting, that as we do our part, He takes care of the rest, now and in eternity.

CHAPTER 9 – QUESTIONS

1. Why do you think Satan wants to steal your inheritance so badly?

2. What does "Putting in the effort" mean for you, when it comes to your relationship with God?

3. What are some of the adversary's schemes that he uses against you?

SESSION 9 – VIDEO QUESTIONS

1. When Jesus said, "The ruler of this world is coming, but he has found nothing in Me," what do you think He meant?

2. Why do you think pride is such a hindrance to our relationship with God?

3. When we take the humble position, it allows God to lift us up. What are some practical ways we can practice and embrace true humility?

Chapter 10 – God's Inheritance

I
t may surprise you to hear that God has an inheritance, but He does! God's inheritance, like ours, consists of a people, a place, and a purpose. Unlike our inheritance, the Father's is not by sonship, it is just because it is. That makes sense considering He is the I am that I am! Though the Father does not have a nachal part of an inheritance He has had to do a whole lot of yarashing! Because of Satan's rebellion and man's choice to rebel there has been something even for God to overcome, our sin!

In order to see God's inheritance, we have to stand back and look at some big picture things, starting at the beginning of time. God created the world for man to dwell in and have fellowship with Him. The world was to be under man's dominion, flowing from God's throne in heaven as Ruler of the Universe. God in turn would enjoy a relationship with humanity as a father to His children. The original people of God's inheritance was to be all of mankind, the place, the heavens and the earth, and the purpose was for God to have a family to share His Kingdom with.

Satan, interrupted all that when he enticed Eve and Adam to question God and ultimately disobey Him. After the fall, God did not sit idly by and only wish for what He had intended for Himself and His children. He put a plan in motion that He had in His heart before the world was created. He began to yarash, that which was meant for Him and mankind!

THERE IS A WAR

Because we don't easily see it with our natural eyes, I think we sometimes forget there has been a war going on in the spiritual realm since Satan rebelled against God. Similar to the wars of human history, theirs is also over, places, people, and whose purposes will prevail in the earth, who will win the inheritance! It should be no surprise to you, if Satan wants to possess your inheritance, he wants God's too! Satan wants to rule God's territory of the heavens and the earth, he wants His position as Ruler over them and the power that comes with it.

> *How you are fallen from heaven, O Lucifer,*
> *son of the morning! How you are cut down to*
> *the ground, You who weakened the nations!*
> *For you have said in your heart: 'I will ascend*
> *into heaven, I will exalt my throne above the*
> *stars of God; I will also sit on the mount of the*
> *congregation On the farthest sides of the*
> *north; I will ascend above the heights of the*
> *clouds, I will be like the Most High."*
> *(Isa. 14:12-14, NKJV)*

The people of the ancient world very often acknowledged the supernatural realm and the battles they contain. In the Old Testament, God is often referred to as the "The Lord of Hosts", or "The Lord of Heaven's Armies." As the Israelites were about to go to war against Jericho, many believe it was Jesus who appeared to Joshua, and called Himself "The Commander of Heaven's Armies." He tells Joshua, if you want to win your inheritance, listen to my strategy. The militaristic language of the Old Testament is purposeful and accurate because the battle over inheritances are real! We are natural people living on the earth, affected by the spiritual battle that is raging around us. That battle is over inheritance, yours and God's.

A BEACHHEAD

Where there is a war, there must be a strategy for victory.
Establishing a beachhead is a tried and true method for
advancing your battle plans. A beachhead is the first piece of
land claimed by an invading force, usually on a shoreline. Once
claimed and defended it's from the beachhead that the invading
army can bring in more soldiers and supplies for the purpose of
expanding their position and gaining more territory. After the
fall of mankind, God chose the tiny nation of Israel to be the
place of His inheritance and the beachhead for His battle
campaign.

> *O God, the nations have come into Your*
> *inheritance; Your holy temple they have*
> *defiled; They have laid Jerusalem in heaps.*
> *(Psa. 79:1, NKJV)*

> *And first I will recompense their iniquity*
> *and their sin double; because they have*
> ***defiled my land, they have filled mine***
> ***inheritance*** *with the carcasses of their*
> *detestable and abominable things.*
> *(Jer. 16:18, KJV)*

God could have called any nation or people group He wanted
to, to live in the land of His inheritance, to share His Kingdom
with, His word, and His ways. Instead of calling a large,
established mighty people, He called out one man and his wife,
and gave them the promise of redemption.

> *When the Most High divided to the nations*
> *their inheritance, when he separated the sons*
> *of Adam, he set the bounds of the people*
> *according to the number of the children of*

Israel. For the LORD's portion is his people;
Jacob is the lot of his inheritance*.*
(Deut. 32:8-9, NKJV)

*'Yet they are **Your people and Your***
***inheritance**, whom You brought out by Your*
mighty power and by Your outstretched arm.'
(Deut. 9:29, NKJV)

THE ELEMENT OF SURPRISE

God chose the small, insignificant family of Abraham to be the people of His inheritance in the earth. This is the glory of God. He takes what seems impossible and He makes it possible, that's also called the element of surprise!

Since the beginning, Satan has only seen in part what God has been doing in human history. Satan heard God's promise to crush his head with a woman's seed, but how could God defeat him using a woman who doesn't even have a seed? Satan heard God's promise to Abraham for many descendants and a land, but how was that going to happen through two barren old people? Satan heard God's promise to the Hebrews for the land of Israel as an inheritance. But how could a bunch of slaves in Egypt defeat giants?

Though Satan has tried and tried to stop God's redemption/inheritance plan, he has not. Satan depends on people operating by what they can see, while God looks for people who will live by what they CAN NOT see! When we act in faith instead of what is seen, it surprises the enemy every time. Satan cannot comprehend our faith in who God is, because he doesn't have it! It's through our faith God's battles are won!

God has always had a remnant of people like Abraham, Moses, Joshua, Deborah, Gideon, and David, who will follow God based on what He says, not what they see. Satan thought he won when the people wouldn't enter the land under Moses, but then God raised up Joshua. Satan thought he took down Israel's monarchy when King Saul failed to put God first, but God had already chosen David in his place. Satan thought he won when Judah and Israel were conquered and dispersed among the nations, but God moved the heart of Gentile Kings to release the people back to the land. Satan thought He won when the Romans ruled Judea, but then a baby boy was born of a virgin girl in the land of Bethlehem, Jesus, The Son of God, The Son of Man. Satan thought he won, when that same Jesus hung on the cross, but then... He conquered the grave!

> *But we speak the wisdom of God in a mystery, the hidden wisdom which God ordained before the ages for our glory, which none of the rulers of this age knew; for had they known, they would not have crucified the Lord of glory.(1 Cor. 2:7-8, NKJV)*

If Satan knew what was going on, he would have never stirred people to kill Jesus! Satan couldn't understand that brute force wouldn't win the war over inheritances. Surprise! It was the humility of our God that won the battle of the ages! By killing Jesus, the Devil played right into God's plan. The earth and man's redemption were won not through a warring king but a sinless Lamb.

> *...the mystery which has been hidden from ages and from generations, but now has been revealed to His saints. (Col. 1:26, NKJV)*

Jesus' birth, life, death, burial and resurrection were the secret plan in the heart of God before the world began! Once again, a man had the right to rule and reign on the earth. This is why I call the New Testament, Inheritance 2.0. In the fullness of time, God sent His Son, to and through the nation of His inheritance to secure man's redemption. Redemption and inheritance do go hand in hand! Jesus's completed work has made a way for the Holy Spirit to come into the earth, empowering believers to stand in the victory that Jesus won over sin and Satan. From the tiny beachhead nation, the gospel of salvation has spread across the earth for the last two thousand years. God's strategy for establishing the beachhead in the land of Israel to regain His inheritance in you and I worked and the enemy didn't even see it coming!

THE TIME IN BETWEEN

Even though Jesus' redemption work is final and complete, we are still living in what I call the time in between. Let me explain, during Jesus' earthly life He yarashed all that God had for Him. That's why from the cross He said, "It is finished." Hebrews says He obtained it, meaning it was something He accomplished during His life.

> *...having become so much better than the angels, as He has **by inheritance obtained** a more excellent name than they*
> *(Heb. 1:4, NKJV)*

Though Jesus accomplished all that He was supposed to during His life on earth, we do not see Him receiving the fullness of His inheritance until the end of the age. Hebrews again speaks about that:

What is man that You are mindful of him,
Or the son of man that You take care of him?
You have made him a little lower than the
angels; You have crowned him with glory and
honor, And set him over the works of Your
hands. You have put all things in subjection
under his feet." For in that He put all in
subjection under him, He left nothing that is
not put under him. ***But now we do not yet see***
all things put under him. *(Heb. 2:6-8, NKJV)*

I would define the time in between as "It's done, but not fully received." The time in between, is the time in between what we do in this life and what we will receive as an inheritance at the end of the age. I believe that just like Jesus, what we are willing to yarash in this life will affect our experience in the Kingdom age.

As I have tried to highlight throughout this study, what we do in this life matters. If Jesus had stayed in Heaven, or decided in the garden He couldn't go through with the cross, would He have gained His nachal inheritance as King of the nations, promised to Him by the Father in Psalm 2?

If what Jesus did in His life mattered, then what we do in ours also matters. I believe at the end of the age, our nachal, or the sonship portion of our inheritance includes right standing with God and eternal life in His Kingdom. The yarash portion will be in the form of rewards we will receive for what we did in this life with what God gave us.

*...since you know that you will **receive an***
inheritance from the Lord as a reward. *It is*
the Lord Christ you are serving.
(Col. 3:24, NIV)

For the Son of Man is going to come in his
Father's glory with his angels, and then he
will reward each person according to what
they have done. *(Matt. 16:27, NIV)*

Look, I am coming soon! **My reward is with**
me, *and I will give to each person according to*
what they have done. (Rev 22:12, NIV)

Jesus, Israel, you, and I are all the same in that there is a portion of our inheritance in this life that we have to get up and go get, we have to yarash! Jesus had to leave His place in heaven to come and claim His inheritance, likewise we must lay claim of ours. God is still the Commander of Heaven's armies, but now He is also the Lord of an army that lives on the earth! We are on the earth for the purpose of carrying out the mission that Jesus started. We are to share the gospel message increasing the Kingdom in the hearts of men until He returns. While our faith won't stop the enemy from trying to fill our inheritance with giants, our faith will make room for God to kick them out!

For whatsoever is born of God overcometh
the world: and this is the victory that
overcometh the world, even our faith.
(1 John 5:4, KJV)

AWAKEN TO YOUR INHERITANCE

Though I had taught on our inheritance many times, and had written most of this book by the Fall of 2018, I still didn't have a title that I liked. As writing was coming to a close, I really began to ask the Lord, "What is the title supposed to be?" Soon after asking, the Lord gave me what I needed. During that season, our family was attending a vibrant church in the heart of Nashville, The Belonging Company. We were in worship, and the presence of the Lord was tangible. As I was lost in adoration of the beauty of the Lord, he whispered to me, "Awaken." I knew immediately that it was the word I was looking for to describe what God wanted to say to the church concerning our inheritance. A few months later, again at The Belonging Company, the Lord confirmed the word to me as Pastor Alex Seeley passionately shared the word God gave her for 2019, awaken.

Awaken means to be drawn into the discovery of something. It means to have your interest aroused. This is my prayer and I believe God's desire, that you will begin to awaken to the portion of the things that God has for you in this life and the next! I pray that you have begun to envision the places, purposes, and people that God wants you to influence for the sake of the gospel and His Kingdom. I pray that you would know the calling that He has for you and walk worthy of it. I pray that you have begun to see what a privilege it is to be called a child of God and the grandness of the things that come with belonging to His family. I pray that you know that God is with you, that He loves you, that He is greater than the best dad you could hope for or imagine. I pray that you have begun to Awaken to Your Inheritance!

Chapter 10 – Questions

1. Based on Ephesians 1:18 Paul prayed that *"......the eyes of your heart may be enlightened in order that you may know the hope to which God has called you, the riches of His glorious inheritance in his holy people."* How do you think the hope to which God has called us connects with the glorious inheritance He has in us?

2. Since God is sovereign, why do you think He lets Satan continue his schemes since He could stop him once and for all at any time?

3. How do you picture it in your mind when God awards to everyone (including Himself) their inheritances at the end of the age?

SESSION 10 – VIDEO QUESTIONS

1. The children of Israel allowed compromise to draw their hearts away from God which ultimately lost them the ability to live in the land of their inheritance. In what ways do you think compromise has the ability to steal, from not only your inheritance, but also God's inheritance in you?

2. What are some areas in your life you struggle to stay out of compromise?

3. Now at the end of our study can you begin to describe the things that your inheritance contains in this life?

4. What are some actions that God is stirring in you to yarash your inheritance?

About The Author

Lynndey grew up in church, and though she had a sincere faith in God, she didn't know how to live a life free from the traps of sin. As a young woman she went very far from God. At her lowest time she heard a man testify that through studying the Bible every day, his whole life changed. In that moment the Holy Spirit prompted her to make the same commitment.

Over the next few years, from the secret place in her living room, God transformed her from the inside out. Not only did she acquire a love for the word, but the Lord gave her insights and revelations for daily living. A few years later, God called her to begin teaching.

Lynndey feels called to those that were once like her, who believe in God but don't know how to live the awesome life Jesus said we could have. It's Lynndey's desire to propel people into living their best life by knowing God through His word.

Lynndey and her husband Chris of 21 years live in the Nashville area with their 4 children and 1 daughter-in-law. Lynndey, also co-hosts The Springs + Roots Podcast, conversations on life and faith. She earned her Bachelors of Theology from Christian Life School of Theology, and enjoys the apostolic fellowship of Maranatha Ministerial Fellowship International.

Made in the USA
Middletown, DE
26 August 2020